OUR IMPASSIONED CALLING

FINDING GOD'S WILL
FOR HIS CHURCH

By

Mark T. Davies

Published November 2005

C.

British Library Cataloguing-In-Publication Data
A Record of This Publication is available from the British Library

ISBN 1905363761

First Published November 2005 by Exposure Publishing,
an imprint of Diggory Press
Three Rivers, Minions, Liskeard, Cornwall, PL14 5LE
WWW.DIGGORYPRESS.COM

CONTENTS

FOREWORD

I will begin exactly where I mean to end. I urge you to pray for the renewal of the Church in these terms:

> Lord God, your purposes!
> Jesus Christ, your passion!
> Holy Spirit, your power!

The book contains reflections on Christian calling in the light of Scripture, history and present-day experience. But the primary reason for writing is not to offer my own reflections. It is to describe how I have found God speaking into my prayers and impressing me with the strength and urgency of his summons, that we should seek his will for his Church.

As a matter of personal gratitude I thank my wife Heather for the life we've shared as well as for the benefit of her judgement in improving what I've here written.

Mark Davies,
York,
November 2005

1. THE PURPOSE OF GOD

Hearing God speak

LATE one Sunday afternoon in the mid-1970s, as minister of a Methodist church in Worcester, I was at home doing final preparation for the evening service. My sermon would be based on the Easter story found in chapter 21 of John's Gospel and especially the record there of Jesus' conversation with Simon Peter. But as I sat at my desk a sudden impression came across my mind. 'Abandon everything you have prepared and when the time comes to preach just say simply what Jesus has done for you'.

Clear as the impression was I did not act on it. I managed to suppress its demand out of nervousness in acting on an impulse. Very likely I believed that my intended message was straightforward and Jesus-centred in any case. So I followed my service order and in the sermon I spoke as I had planned, probably making three points as preachers often do.

Standing at the front of the church during that service I saw that in addition to many usual attenders there was a young man at the back whom I did not recognise at all. In conversation afterwards he said he had decided to come to church that evening because there was currently a lot of difficulty in his life. I asked him whether being at the service had felt all right and whether what I'd said had been any use to him. He replied with unembarrassed honesty that he had paid no attention to my preaching at all. He said, 'I sat there and wished someone would get up and simply say what Jesus had done for them'.

Over some weeks and months we did get to know him. The contact with the church had meaning for him. He felt that God was actually at work in his life and some of the pain was being sorted. Life did open up afresh for him. But the point of telling the story here is that on that initial Sunday evening God did speak to me. Of course this does not devalue the labour that is normally required in preparation or suggest that preaching should usually take the form of straight individual testimony. But in this case there was a plain way for one person to be reached and the rest of the congregation would have survived it. There was evidence of God's profound love for a particular seeking individual contained within the 'crowd', something which the Gospel record of the ministry of Jesus frequently illustrates.

7

From experiences of my own through the last thirty years and from very many experiences recorded by others I have learned more about listening to God in this mysterious way that comes through impression. Of course we should recognise what purely human elements may be at work. To be proved right in one instance does not necessarily mean being right next time. We do need to be guarded against making mistakes that can affect others. This sort of guidance should not be emphasised at the expense of standard ways of God's leading - obedience to main truths of Scripture, rational thought processes and sharing the insights of others.

Yet it can be an authentic way in which God communicates. The New Testament regards prophetic sorts of inspiration as an ongoing stream in the Church's life. Paul's familiar advice is 'Don't quench the Spirit, don't despise prophetic messages, but test everything; keep the good, avoid evil of whatever kind' (1 Thess. 5.19-22).

Working in a church in Devon in the 1990s I suggested a date when the church might be open all day for people to come in and pray quietly for whatever length of time they chose. When I went myself to spend some time there on that morning I suddenly felt God was speaking with a directness I had not anticipated, telling me to encourage the church to a longer period of time which would be specially marked by prayer.

Leave no stone unturned to rouse others that they should seek my face and call to me, 'We have so little of which to boast unless you help us'. Stir a great cry to rise from people's hearts saying, 'O Lord, set your presence here, because without you we are nothing'.

Over the next weeks I did as well as I could with the stirring. By speaking and writing I encouraged everyone in the church to pray seriously: 'This is your work, so please do it'. I encouraged them to ask for God's presence and help in as heartfelt a way as they were able. After a certain time I distinctly believed that, however imperfect our corporate response might have been, there had nevertheless been a response and God had accepted it. Of course it would be right for people to go on praying as a constant ingredient of Christian life. But over this period we had followed a specific leading.

We were not in a visibly helpless state. For several years, beginning well before our own arrival, there had been considerable new life and growth based on the influx of new population into the area. There had been incorporation of many young adults of varying church backgrounds into a long-standing Methodist community. Plenty of prayer as well as energy had already gone into its recent development. But here was a fresh and particular call to acknowledge God's personal sovereignty over the church's life.

It is not right to measure quality of obedience according to quickly visible results. However, I do think that the strength and character of the church's further development, both before and after we left it ourselves, has been a result of God's purposeful engagement with people who have called out to him.

Over recent years I have frequently felt that God was speaking through times of prayer. When my wife and I pray together we typically end with a few moments of just being quiet and asking God to show us something if he wishes. We readily accept it when nothing particular occurs. But often sequences of words have come into my mind that seemed spontaneous, as something heard rather than devised. These have sometimes corresponded with visual impressions which came to my wife, not full-scale visions but clear and unexpected mental images.

Before proceeding further I would like to write briefly about my Christian experience from the beginning. This will help in the understanding of personal illustrations throughout the book. The free use of reminiscence is not for claiming any self-importance over against the experience of others. Whoever we are and whatever our story to date we all need humble and seeking attitudes.

A personal background

The memorial to Karl Marx in London's Highgate Cemetery is surmounted by a massive carving of his head. Along its length is inscribed the rallying-cry of the Communist manifesto, 'Workers of the world, unite! You have nothing to lose but your chains'. By contrast the obscure grave I had gone to see was marked by a simple stone cross and a verse from the Psalms. 'With thee is the fountain of life and in thy light we shall see light' (Psalm 36.9)

My great-grandmother died in 1888 at the age of 39. From reminiscences written down by my grandfather I happened to know that his mother was buried in Highgate. He said that the verse on her grave was from the Psalm prescribed by her daily Bible readings on

9

the day when she died. Some time in the 1980s I paid a quick visit. In such a vast expanse of burials it was remarkably close to the burial-place of Marx, one of the cemetery's most famous names.

Like Marx my great-grandmother had come to live in London from Germany. Unlike his negative boyhood experience of religion, with a father who exchanged Judaism for Lutheranism for the sake of business advantage, she had grown up in a family environment which brought her into Christian conviction. She had come to a Conference in Brighton that drew young Christians from various parts of Europe and while there had met a Scotsman with whom she afterwards corresponded and eventually married.

'With you is the fountain of life and in your light we shall see light'. This is the expression of a hope in God relevant to both living and dying. It characterised not only this particular great-grandmother but many of my family members in previous generations including all four of my grandparents and my own father and mother.

I grew up in the Methodist Church and throughout my teens had a definite belief in God's reality and a conviction that I would enter the ministry. As a University student I was particularly keen on the social dimensions of the Gospel and got involved with other young Christians in practical projects in needy areas of my home city of Birmingham.

In my third year at University, partly as a result of studying philosophy, I began to experience severe doubts, for the first time uncertain of whether there could be a personal God at all and realising with honesty that I hardly knew the meaning of 'salvation' as described with enthusiasm by New Testament authors. In the course of time the doubting became less acute and I received encouragement from others that a measure of doubt was quite in order as an ongoing ingredient of Christian life. So I pursued my way into training for the church's ministry.

During two years of training, at the end of the 1960s, I maintained a deep interest in the study of the Bible, especially the New Testament. I believed in God but without any personal practice of prayer. I was particularly impressed by the passage in John's Gospel where many of Jesus' followers desert him and he says to the intimate circle of the Twelve, 'Will you also go away?' Simon Peter answered, 'Lord, to whom shall we go? You have the words of eternal life' (John 6.68). In this passage Peter goes on to an affirmation that

Jesus is the Messiah. But the phrase that was specially meaningful to me at this period was the simple question, 'Lord, to whom shall we go?' Even in youthful struggle and uncertainty it was real to me that I did not know a better option for life than was somehow wrapped up in the message and person of Jesus.

I was given the opportunity to go abroad for a year at a German university instead of doing a third year of training in this country. Here, in the summer of 1971, something happened which I will describe further ahead. Impressed by a student Christian group I came into a new period of heart-searching, emerging in a wonderful assurance of being known and loved by God through Jesus. The effect of this was that God seemed no longer primarily an idea, whether believed or doubted. Without pride or pretension I knew that I knew him and I started to live in a relationship of love with him.

Returning to England I started a two-year appointment as a 'probationer' minister. I became interested in the worship and teaching events held at a nearby venue in Dorset by a local Christian community. The charismatic style of worship, the many references to the Holy Spirit and his gifts and the overall sense of being part of a sweeping worldwide movement which God was creating in our own time - all these were in my experience considerably new elements. From that time onwards I have drawn much help and inspiration from streams of Christian life that would broadly be called charismatic.

But even in using a word such as 'charismatic' I register my dislike of labels. Nowhere in what I write is my intention to magnify one or other particular label. All Christians are called to keep on discovering more of the full dimensions of the New Testament witness. Paul's prayer in the Letter to the Ephesians is: 'May you, in company with all God's people, be strong to grasp what is the breadth and length and height and depth of Christ's love, and to know it, though it is beyond knowledge' (3.18,19).

Love God, love his purposes

In 2003 I was in the fourth year of an appointment in Derbyshire. My wife and I came into a period of time when constantly in our prayers we believed God was speaking about his desire to control and direct the life of his Church. The things written down in this period apply beyond the life of any single local church to the Church as a whole.

God says, 'Love me, love my purposes'.

Sometimes what God calls for in the life of the Church is like the ministry of John the Baptist except there is no river. There is a spiritual stream into which people can choose to step saying, 'Lord, make me personally ready for what you want to bring, whatever it means'.

Some of the words written down speak of God's judgement on the life of the Church, even though it is a judgement expressed in love. It is God's prerogative to speak about the Church in judgement. In no way do I feel judgemental myself about whatever sins, contradictions or shortcomings in the life of churches have made us less than God wanted us to be. I have my own share in them and am not in the least self-satisfied with what I have been or done. For all of us the past is under the mercy of God but the future is open to his direction.

The Church is a jungle of contradictions, so much good and so much evil, so much looking to God and so much looking away. People need to be taught a plain path and a plain purpose, which is to glorify him.

Sometimes God comes to the Church just looking for a way in, like a man who runs along the length of a wall hoping there will be a crack to squeeze through, a way to get to the other side. But sometimes there is barely enough opening to look through, let alone to get in.

Sometimes the Church is like a garment so ripped and shredded that it is nothing like a design of God's making.

Some of the words strongly express God's desire for Christians to offer him back control. Closely associated with this is God's promise of blessing.

God says to the Church, You can become a people so greatly blessed when you just take your hands off from holding on so tightly and instead say, 'Lord, do as you wish, do as you please, do as you purpose'.

The promises that God sets before people require so little, only a yes to his doing it, only lips shaped to say Yes and not No.

God wants to break the power of human control in the life of the Church. People must entrust to him what is on the other side of the loss of control.

As I now write down some of these sentences for the reflection of others it is easy for me to want to qualify them. 'Breaking the power of human control' cannot deny the normal importance of healthy standards of responsibility and efficiency, foresight and planning. Many churches can be glad of democratic elements in their running, with a strong emphasis placed on participation, as well as an essential role for good leadership, rightly based on the earning and retaining of trust. We must affirm the freedom which the New Testament regularly presupposes. It is perfectly allowed that Christians will often simply make choices, believing that if the overall intention of their lives is to honour God then he will work with them in and through their choices and through all other eventualities.

And yet I don't want to clutter these sentences with qualifications. Here as often in the Bible I find God speaking in straight and strong terms, even in terms that can initially seem strange and paradoxical. He calls us to acknowledge truths that get overlaid by our own handling of affairs. He has his own plans and intentions. There is a heart-attitude to God which truly allows him sovereignty and gives him back permission to do as he wants.

God knows that we do not have perfect wisdom in understanding him and the routes he wants to take us, whether individually or corporately in the life of churches.

God wants people to offer him permission to do as he pleases, saying 'Lord, help us to know what is of you. Have respect to our own fear, frailty and uncertainty. Condescend to who we are. Accommodate yourself to the level of our seeing. We pray for the gift of recognition, to recognise you when you call, speak, stand among us'.

God wants to stress the desire to please him, even where people feel they don't know exactly what pleases him. They are to cry, 'Show us what is pleasing to you'. God searches people's hearts and clears a way for himself. Beyond the time of calling and searching God will come in with grace, tenderness, compassion, intimacy and innermost experience.

Many Christians feel more or less comfortably settled with the level of their own faith. They have their own ideas about what they would like to be the particular features and the particular future of the church to which they belong, whether at the local or wider level. These are shaped by many factors of individuality and experience. Yet God is calling all of us to reach out to him afresh. He is above and beyond the limitations of our perception to date, above and beyond the insistence of our own attitudes.

In calling us to seek him I believe that God emphasises his power to make us the people he wants us to be.

God wants to proclaim freedom to many whose experience has been inhibited. Perhaps they have lived in his Church since they were small. They know the first commandment, 'Love God with all your heart....' But now the breath of his Holy Spirit will come on them and enable them to do it. And to love their neighbours as they love themselves.

God calls from heaven for movements of the heart which say, 'Yes, Lord, what you want to find in us, create in us. For you are our God and we are your people'.

The scope of the book

It might be judged that the sense of hearing God speak is a phenomenon of my subconscious mind out of years of engagement with the Bible and with Christian thinking. I have continually attempted to allow God control of my own life. I have been constantly involved with tasks of ministry and preaching. I have been familiar with churches where 'hearing from God' was accepted and taught.

Yet repeatedly what has come in prayer has seemed different in style and content from what I would have thought to express. Later on there is a chapter which more fully considers the place of prophecy in Christian experience. I am personally convinced about hearing from God in the instances I have given. But I don't want to try too hard to argue for it. Where impressions originally came as a sense of God's speaking in the first person I have changed them to a third person form.

The themes which came to me so strongly in my prayers in 2003 can be summarised in a Trinitarian way. The transcendent God calls us to seek his purposes. He calls us to respond with passion to the passionate character of Jesus' mission. He calls us to find empowering through his Holy Spirit.

It is in historic churches as well as those of newer growth that the purposes of God are still to be worked out. In the course of 2004 I had a particular sense of God's love and desire for the Methodist Church in Britain. Although this book is written without any intention of denominational restriction it includes one chapter that does specially consider Methodism.

While preparing this book I've also had time to read more of what others have written. I was specially interested by 'Red Moon Rising', which describes the growth of the '24-7' prayer movement.[1] I have looked at other recent books which address the current situation of the churches in Britain, books which recognise the seriousness of the statistics of decline but also find many signs of Christians responding to current opportunities with courage and creativity. They offer their own challenges to new possibilities and while refusing easy optimism they express a vital hope.[2]

One example of these is called 'Hope for the Church', written by an Anglican called Bob Jackson. It has much reference to the Church of England but plenty of relevance to all churches. It contains many suggestions for appropriate ways and means of growth even in current circumstances.

This present book does mention God from time to time, and it assumes that good Christians will continue to pray as though prayer was all that mattered. But primarily it urges Christians to use our God-given intelligence to analyse our situation logically, and so to seek out the pathways for growth that God has already excavated, and some have pioneered.[3]

I wholly agree with the use of God-given intelligence and I admire the book's detailed practical wisdom. Its God-centred passion is in fact clearly apparent.

15

The church that satisfies postmoderns in their search for real spirituality will allow God to be himself - the giant and glorious Trinitarian mystery, never properly encompassed, always unpredictable and available to be explored afresh.[4]

What I've written is small in scale but offers my own reflection on the giant and glorious Trinitarian mystery. I mention God continually and write about prayer explicitly.

Here is one more impression that came out of praying:

God calls people to say, 'Let us never again talk of the life of the Church as a thing in itself, only about the Lord, present, active, merciful'.

2. THE PASSION OF JESUS

Conversations over pizza

ANNIKA was in her twenties when we got to know her. Her faith was visible in her life and character. Describing how she had became a Christian she said that her family had never gone to church. She grew up with no experience of Christianity ever being a matter of conversation. When she was thirteen she had a schoolfriend who often said 'It's so good at our church, you must come'. And she would reply 'I don't think so'. But the other girl kept inviting her relentlessly until finally she replied, 'I will come just once on condition you never talk to me about it again'.

So she went on a Sunday and she thought the worship time and the singing were very beautiful. She started to cry and she cried quietly all through the rest of the service. Next Sunday and every Sunday through the following weeks she kept returning. She listened to what was said and things began to fall into place. There is a God who is real. His love is personal. He sent Jesus to live and die for us. It is possible to say Yes to him and live in a relationship of love with him.

We know the immense variety of individual journeys in Christian faith. This happened to be hers. Whether or not a person is nurtured in the life of the church for their first twelve years is not the main issue. Transmission of faith from parents to children has a key place in God's purposes but even so faith has to be discovered and appropriated for ourselves.

British Churches intended that the 1990s should be a special decade for outreach. In 1991 I joined several hundred others at a conference in London under the title of 'Church Leadership in the Decade of Evangelism'. I was there on my own and when it came to teatime the first day I spotted someone else who looked solitary and asked if he wanted to find something to eat.

He was a young Nigerian on a short visit to England and he was a pastor of a church in the city of Ibadan. We ordered a large pizza and divided it between us. I asked how big his church was and he said 3000 people. As though concerned that might sound on the small side he added, 'But it's growing fast'. He was currently one of five pastors. He told me about the large meetings for worship and the small meetings for close fellowship.

17

At one point I asked him if there were many Muslims in Ibadan. He said there were and that a considerable number of Muslims came to their church. Often they had started to come of their own accord, saying they'd had dreams and visions of Jesus and wanted to know more about him. There had been no attempt at organised evangelism in Muslim communities. But many Muslims had become Christians and gone back to bring other family members to church. The church had recently appointed a new pastor from this background.

On the following day I thought that I would try the same and have another half-pizza for my tea. I saw someone else who was standing around on his own and invited him to come to the cafe I already knew. He was a young man who said he'd been a Christian only a short while. Someone had invited him to the Conference and he'd enjoyed being there. He was amazed by the number of people and the sense of vitality.

His story was that he had travelled all over the country as a musician, playing the guitar with a group and what he called 'getting into scrapes'. At some point he found that his sister had become a Christian. Whenever he saw her he tried to tease her about it or be sarcastic, but really he was impressed by the change in her. He tried himself to pray a prayer of commitment to God but didn't feel much effect.

Many more months had gone by and he had found himself in some situation that felt desperate to him at the time. In the solitude of his room he had called out, 'Oh God, if you're real, please show yourself'. At this point he leaned towards me over the table and said seriously, 'I don't know if you'll believe this'. What had happened was that he saw Jesus walk into the room. Jesus had not spoken but had just stood with a gesture of his hand indicating, 'I'm here if you need me'.

The vision had quickly disappeared but had left him amazed. Life continued. But gradually his perception was that in some radical way his life had altered on the inside. He found a church to attend – I am not sure what denomination – and had persevered in going even though he didn't feel specially welcome. He was aware of a strong impulse somehow to reach out to people in the culture which he knew and find right ways of expressing what he had found. He said he had lived for years with nobody in any circumstance ever telling him anything about Jesus.

It was coincidental that visions of Jesus featured in both these conversations. It can be wonderful when God communicates in such ways. But it must not be implied that seeing Jesus in vision is a superior way of knowing him. In John's Gospel Jesus pronounces a special Easter blessing on the overwhelming majority of his future disciples when he says 'Happy are those who have not seen me and yet have believed' (John 20.29).

I did not keep contact with either of these men, so I do not know what the further passage of years may have brought for them. Both in their own way were passionate witnesses to the living reality of Jesus. Both were rather quiet in manner so we are not talking about a passion expressed in voluble terms. But they spoke with the depth of feeling that comes from engagement with God himself and the sense of immense preciousness in being a disciple of Jesus and extending the knowledge of him to others.

Authentic passion

In the first chapter I described a period of time that was full of impressions of God addressing his Church. Frequently there were expressions of his delight in the qualities of Christian character.

It is a great thing to the Lord to see hearts submitted to him, to hear the sounds of hearts attuned to his heart, to taste their flavour.

The Lord has determined that not by power or might, natural ability, superfluity of energy, wealth, health or optimism - by none of these things will he bring in his Kingdom. His purpose is fixed to bring it in through those who acknowledge his holiness and are humble in spirit.

God is hungry for hearts that know him, minds that love him, wills that serve him, strength of endeavour to pursue him. God calls his people to a combination of qualities, a specific character string. Passion. Peace. Purity. Empowerment. Hope.

The theme of 'passion' or 'zeal' seemed to be recurrent.
There are a lot of people in the Church in whose hearts God finds a basic pattern of righteousness but he doesn't find zeal. He doesn't find what is described in the Book of Hosea – 'Come,

let us press on, let us strive to know the Lord' (6.3). God longs for something so winning, so attractive to be presented to them that they would spontaneously say, 'Don't let us stay where we are in the knowledge of God. We've already submitted to God. Now let us strive to know him more'.

God engages intimately with his Church when it says to others, 'Jesus is the Bread of Life. Without him we perish'. The Church should see itself as though surrounded by crowds of spiritually starving, emaciated people. The Church questions God: 'How may we reach this multitude?' God answers, 'Not by a plan but by a passion'.

I know that planning must have its place in outreach. So I interpret 'not that but this' to mean 'this is more important than that'. God calls for the passionate recognition that people actually need him.

'Passion' and 'passionate' are words in frequent general use for all sorts of convictions and enthusiasms. We can notice them repeatedly when we read newspapers or watch television.

Of course Christianity has always involved passion. Christians believe that Jesus is unique in his person and his work, unique in his relationship with God and unique in his revealing and reconciling work from God to human beings. He was also truly human and he is the model for our own humanity. From the Sermon on the Mount and from the Gospel record in its entirety we are to absorb the whole range of values which his teaching and his character present. But a particular overarching quality of his teaching and character may be described as zeal or passion. John tells us that when Jesus drove traders out of the Jerusalem temple his disciples remembered Old Testament words, 'Zeal for your house will consume me' (John 2.17).

This use of the word passion in relation to Jesus is of course distinct from the traditional use of the same word in relation to Jesus' suffering and death. Passion defined as suffering is different from passion defined as the sway of strong feeling. And yet in the case of Jesus a powerful link is present between both meanings. The unified direction of his ministry is summed up when he says, 'The Son of Man did not come to be served but to serve – and to give his life as a ransom for many' (Mark 10.45). Christians find the passionate love of God for humanity supremely revealed where Jesus endures unqualified rejection on the Cross.

20

There are theologians in all periods of the Church's history who have brought a quality of passion to their thinking. Some have reflected on passion explicitly as a theme of theology, including Soren Kierkegaard in Denmark who devoted himself to a life of thought and writing until his early death in 1855. He attacked the superficiality of the nominal Christianity practised in the Lutheran state church and looked for a faith that involved costly personal commitment.

The work of a German theologian called Jurgen Moltmann has related strongly both to the Trinity and to the subject of passion. 'Christian faith lives from a great passion and is itself the passion for life which is prepared for suffering'.[1] Moltmann himself as a young man became a Christian by gradual process as he wrestled with issues of suffering in his first-hand experience of the wartime bombing of his home city of Hamburg as well as the time he spent as a prisoner of war.

Some of Moltmann's reflections are taken up and developed in a book called 'Practicing Passion', published in 2004 by a lively theologian of American youth culture called Kenda Creasy Dean. 'A passionless church will never address passionate youth. It is highly questionable whether a passionless church addresses anybody, or if it is even the church in the first place. Christianity requires passion, and youth know it'.[2]

Christian passion is the felt response to God's self-giving love and life-giving revelation in Jesus. It to be distinguished from any artificial affectation of feelings, a constant use of exaggerated expressions, a glorification of emotion for its own sake. We are not approving one sort of temperament over against another but passion can be expressed in people who are widely different temperamentally and in every way. Authentic passion arises out of preoccupation with God and his call. It is not focused primarily on ourselves and how passionately we are feeling or behaving or worshipping or witnessing.

Authentic passion is to be distinguished from a fearful impression of intensity in everything we say or do. It co-exists well with human normality. It fits with the appreciation of life, its richness and its possibilities. It is clear that Jesus himself who is the model of passionate commitment to God's cause is also our model for continual enjoyment of the world. He is the one who sanctions relaxation and light-heartedness and ordinary things, the company of the meal-table and the special relationships of family and friendship. The passion of Jesus within us leaves latitude for all sorts of things that individually we like, even though it also creates readiness for self-discipline and sacrifice.

Authentic Christian passion is not the fanatical spirit which has frequently made religion a force for intolerance or hostility. We are enabled to reach out to others across whatever differences in creative and generous ways. We long that others would be able to find the reality of Jesus for themselves but this must not be expressed in an offensive or coercive manner.

Authentic passion is not a headlong rush into a state of exhaustion from setting ourselves to be or do more than we can. Jesus says that his yoke is easy and his burden is light. He is not imposing upon us, individually or corporately, an impossible weight of demand. But still he has come to revolutionise us. He calls for a passionate allegiance to himself as the central motivation of our lives. He enables us to give him this allegiance and to experience it as liberating, fulfilling and joy-giving.

God passionately requires passion in his church. Let us not shy away from this out of fear of seeming extreme. Let us not say, 'I am not by nature a passionate person'. God is calling individual Christians and Christian communities to fresh awakenings. He is hungry for passionate responses.

Summer term in Germany

Some more about my own journey in Christian faith. I have mentioned the opportunity which I had in my mid-twenties of spending a year doing New Testament studies at the University of Tubingen. It was altogether a stimulating year. I enjoyed the town and the international character of the University environment. I heard lectures by some outstanding theologians, including the Catholic scholar Hans Kung, and I specially explored what had been written in recent years on the Acts of the Apostles.

There was also a course which I attended on questions of dialogue between Christianity and Marxism. I made a brief and not very successful attempt to learn Spanish because of the interest I felt in the struggles for justice in Latin America.

At the beginning of the year's final term I accepted an invitation from a fellow-Englishman to attend an informal international Christian group which met weekly on Sunday evenings in the room of a German student. The tone was friendly and relaxed and each week a Bible passage was chosen as a basis for conversation. Something developed within me more profound than my Christian commitment to date had yet managed to give me, a sense of excitement, anticipation and awe about encounter with God.

On the first evening I remember being moved by a fragment of the discussion where a girl from Bangor University spoke briefly about her Christian life as a response to the death of Jesus on the Cross. She had seen that the death of Jesus was the answer to her own experience of weakness. I did not exactly understand what she said. But I remember recognising that through a few words spoken in German a forceful blow was being struck somewhere in my own heart.

I made some good friends within this group and spent time with them socially during the weeks of May and June as well as on the Sunday evenings. One of them in particular both annoyed me and fascinated me by his love of God and his general enthusiasm. I remember initially reacting with an element of secret anger to books which he lent me. I felt a touch of offence that I might have been spotted as someone needing encouragement to become a more ardent Christian. They were especially books with a missionary background demonstrating the reality of close personal relationships with God and, along with the acceptance of suffering, a proven confidence in God's capacity to hear and answer prayer. What was the nature of the threat which they presented to me? I believed in God and was willing to believe in the miraculous, at least in a New Testament setting. But I was a complicated person and as human beings we can always feel threatened by God's closer approach.

Any annoyance was soon overlaid by the sense of engagement in a fresh quest. One book impressed me by its special attention to a verse from the Letter to the Hebrews: 'Whoever comes to God must believe that he exists and that he rewards those who seek him' (11.6).[3] I was starting to read the Bible afresh as a matter of personal urgency rather than only as an object of study. I found a gradual capacity to spend time speaking to God in prayer and positively to want to set time aside for this purpose. As a theological student I had never done this, rationalising that the quantity of time I spent in thinking about the Bible and Christian issues amounted to more or less the same thing as praying. To find myself praying in private, first for periods of just a few minutes at a time and then for longer periods, was something to which I was so unused that it felt miraculous in itself. I also experienced some exact answers to practical things I prayed, which I believe were a gracious concession from God in leading me along.

On Sunday evenings totally familiar Bible passages seemed to take on a new depth – Jesus and the Samaritan woman at the well, the parable of the prodigal son, Isaiah chapter 53. It was as though God had never seemed nearer and yet as though even in the closeness there was a sense of obstruction, of a barrier that needed to be removed. I remember that once when I was praying, aware both of God's closeness and of the barrier between us, I felt distinctly as though Jesus was kneeling beside me and that he was keeping company with me on my side of the barrier.

I did not tell others of the acuteness that I was experiencing in my own spiritual search. The end of the University term came close, the last of our Sunday meetings came and I had only ten days left in Germany. On that evening we read the story from Mark chapter 10 about the so-called 'rich young ruler' who came to Jesus and then went away with a heavy heart. Jesus said, 'How hard it is to enter the Kingdom of God'. The disciples were astonished and said, 'Then who *can* be saved?' Jesus looked at them and said, 'With men it is impossible, but not for God; everything is possible with God' (10.26,27).

When the discussion and prayer were over I remember that we stayed together in the room for a long time. No one wanted to go. We liked each other's company. It was a nice experience of Christian friendship.

During the last week of my year abroad I came into a few days of intense longing for a reality of heart-relationship with God that only God could give. I went for long solitary walks in the woods near my lodgings. I recognised that I was going through a process of repentance. This was not experienced as any special regret over particular sins. But it was like a turning away from a life which now seemed essentially controlled by the 'self', towards a life which I could not achieve by effort or well-meaning but which I knew God could give, fully claimed and befriended and ruled by him.

And then one morning I knew this gift had been given. I came into a settled peace in being accepted and loved by God. It seemed so precious that I spontaneously thought, 'Such a thing could not possibly be earned unless it was at an infinite cost'. I saw that an infinite cost had been paid by Jesus and my previous acquaintance with theories of the atonement took on a new light.

There were definite emotions at the time and for weeks and months afterwards but I do not regard it as an 'emotional experience'. It was a total experience bringing a specific conviction of God's reality which I have never lost and a knowledge of the limitless outreach of his love to everyone.

In the immense variety of individual journeys this was part of mine. I do not question that others have found passionate levels of Christian commitment in quite different circumstances, not so obviously by datable events nor through such a struggle. But this was part of my own discovery of Christian passion, the passion in God's heart which elicits response from us.

The commands of Jesus

In a village chapel in 1995 we spent time discussing the tasks of Christ's Church as a whole, as a background to thinking afresh what a local church should look like. There were some good contributions. All those contributions seemed tied together when I mentioned a pre-packaged answer from a book of systematic theology which I had recently bought.[4] This conveniently outlined the purposes of the Church as:

- Ministry to God: Worship
- Ministry to Believers: Nurture
- Ministry to the World : Evangelism and Mercy

The book stressed the importance of all these purposes and of emphasising them continually in a healthy church, although naturally the gifts of individuals might be particularly applied to just one area. A similar kind of outline has since then become familiar from a book by Rick Warren called 'The Purpose-Driven Church', which connects the purposes directly with the words of Jesus in the so-called Great Commandments and Great Commission.[5]

In 2000 the Methodist Church in Britain adopted a statement on 'Our Calling', described in fourfold terms of worship, learning, service and evangelism. It was commended as practical guidance for local churches and Circuits in their reflection on their life and mission.

We can choose to express the Church's purposes in our own phraseology. But our expressions should still be measured against the full force and feeling of the words of Jesus. Jesus uses emphatic language taken from the Old Testament Law when he summarises the Law's requirements in terms of two commands in relation to God and neighbour (Mark 12.28-31).

• The first is the resounding call from the heart of Deuteronomy (6.4,5) : 'Hear O Israel, the Lord your God is one, and you shall love the Lord your God with all your heart, and with all your soul, and with all your mind, and with all your strength' .

• The second is drawn from a passage of detailed instructions in Leviticus (19.18), 'You shall love your neighbour as yourself', which the teaching of Jesus applies radically to generous and caring attitudes and actions towards others without restriction.

In John's account of the Last Supper Jesus also gives that 'new commandment' which is intimate in its reference to the circle of his own disciples and searching in its appeal to Jesus' own example. 'Love one another as I have loved you, that you also love one another' (13.34).

The Great Commission is also a passionate statement, characterised by its repeated use of the word 'all' (Matthew 28.18-20).

• 'Go and make all nations my disciples.'
• 'Teach them to observe all that I have commanded you.'

These large instructions are placed between two unrestricted claims. Jesus has been given 'all authority' in heaven and on earth. His personal presence will be with his followers for always, literally 'all the days'.

The Great Commission is the climax of Matthew's Gospel. How far this is likely to be an exact account of words heard from the lips of the Risen Jesus has been much discussed. But it is clear from the accounts of the original Easter period that Jesus not only appeared to his followers in varied numbers on numerous occasions but conversed with them freely. We should regard the Great Commission as at least

26

a trustworthy summary of the major themes on which he spoke, including the reality of his risen life, his promise of the Holy Spirit and an unambiguous commission to spread his message. An explicit remembered command of the Risen Jesus to baptise explains why baptism was accepted as the practice of the Christian community from its earliest days. The command to go to all nations fulfils the many hints in Jesus' ministry that beyond his own death and resurrection he anticipated the extension of his mission beyond Judaism to the world at large.

My first chapter was about calling to God to do what he wants in our lives and in the life of Christian communities. This surrender and this appeal are open-ended. 'Lord, do as you wish, do as you please, do as you purpose'. But they are in the light of God's revelation through Jesus and the directions which Jesus has given.

God calls his people to a combination of qualities, a specific character string. Passion. Peace. Purity. Empowerment. Hope.

Now we can ask again about empowerment. How are we to be empowered for a life which is measured against the Great Commandments and the Great Commission? What is the nature of this power? How can we be empowered in the way that Jesus intended for us?

3. THE SPIRIT'S EMPOWERING

'What is that?'

THE Holy Spirit can easily be a source of puzzlement. On a Saturday evening in 1971, in the course of the German summer which I've already described, I had been invited to a party at the home of an American couple. It was not a Christian gathering but during the evening somebody happened to comment that the next day was Whit Sunday. Our American host said, 'Remind me, what is Whit Sunday all about?'. On being informed that it was to do with the Holy Spirit he said, 'What is that? I don't understand the concept'.

As a theological student, and in the absence of anyone else wanting to bring enlightenment, I gave a quick answer. I said that Christians ascribe to the Holy Spirit their inner resources for living the Christian life. I referred to Pentecost when the followers of Jesus were conscious of new power for preaching the message about him. Someone interjected his own summary of the Christian message, 'Brothers, Christ died for our sins - shall we make light of his sacrifice and not commit them?' Then he thought of some other jokes he knew. They amused him more than they amused anyone else but they brought an end to serious conversation.

Church people know that Whit Sunday is linked with Pentecost just as Good Friday and Easter are linked with Passover. The Jewish festivals are the historic occasions of the events which Christians commemorate. By comparison with these the story in John's Gospel chapter 7 of Jesus at another festival is less often preached about or specially recalled. Yet John gives considerable space to his account of Jesus' presence at the Feast of Shelters (also called 'Tabernacles') in the last autumn of his life. It is in the setting of this celebration that John records Jesus making a dramatic invitation (7.37-39).

On the last and greatest day of the feast Jesus stood and cried aloud, 'Let anyone who is thirsty come to me, and let the one who believes in me drink. As the scripture has said, 'Out of the believer's heart shall flow rivers of living water'. Now he said this about the Spirit, which believers in him were to receive...

Tabernacles was the very climax of joyful celebration in the Jewish year, also called the Feast of Feasts or the Feast of Joy. It had a harvest significance but also a historic memory of the journey of Israel through the wilderness to the Promised Land. Every day during the festival week water was carried through the streets of Jerusalem and symbolically poured out around the Temple altar. At night huge lamps illuminated the Temple area and there was lively music and dancing. Crowds of people expressed their enthusiasm in celebration of human well-being and a rich spiritual heritage. There was even a saying, 'He who has not seen Jerusalem at the Feast of Tabernacles does not know what joy means'.

Here, as well as at the Passover and Pentecost later to come, the significance of Israel's historic commemoration is transcended by the arrival of Israel's Messiah.

I believe that John accurately testifies to events in Jesus' ministry even where they have also passed through the processes of his own reflection. He supplements the other Gospels by his accounts of Jesus' repeated visits to Jerusalem, often with exact detail of locations or timing. He dramatically conveys the atmosphere at this particular festival when the authorities were already tense about Jesus' activities and planning for his arrest. During the climactic celebration of the final day, standing somewhere in the festival crowd and most likely at a point in the solemn liturgy where silence was being observed, Jesus cried out with a loud voice.[1] He makes an impassioned appeal for individual response. Anyone who knows they are still spiritually thirsty can apply to him for a supreme source of refreshment which will also become a life-giving stream to others. John has reflected on this promise. He applies it to the future activity of the Holy Spirit in the Christian community after Jesus' death and resurrection.

I have already mentioned that after my return from Germany, having embarked on my first appointment in ministry, I became interested in the worship and teaching events held by a charismatic Christian community at Lytchett Minster in Dorset. Having come to know God's love through Jesus in a newly personal way I now developed a sense of fascination with the person and work of the Holy Spirit. For a while it seemed that repeatedly when I opened the Bible it was the name of the Holy Spirit that leapt out at me. But I also appreciated what the teaching at Post Green clearly expressed, that the Spirit's intention is to make Jesus real to us and through us.

Over several months the promise of the Spirit became associated in my mind with three things which I definitely wanted - to live the Christian life with an ongoing sense of joy, to have a clean heart resistant to insidious temptations and to be able to communicate

Christian reality effectively to others. I was deeply impressed by biblical passages about the Spirit, perhaps especially the words of Jesus in John chapter 7 because what I was experiencing felt exactly like an intense thirst.

On the Saturday evening just before Whit Sunday 1972 I was at a meeting at Lytchett Minster. At the end an offer of personal prayer was made. There was a room to which people could go if they wanted to commit their lives to Christ and there was a room for those who wanted to experience more of the Spirit in their Christian lives. I made for the second room where someone prayed with me briefly and quite unemotionally. I felt fairly peaceful and nothing more. I noticed the faces of one or two others who were being prayed with, because I could see a definite radiance around them and I fully believed that the Holy Spirit was present.

I was given a leaflet entitled 'Jesus, the Baptiser in the Holy Spirit' and I drove back to the bedsitter where I was living at the time. I sat down to read the leaflet but an instant impatience came over me about reading or thinking any more on the subject. I started praying aloud to Jesus and words flowed effortlessly of which I did not understand the meaning. As is regularly the case with the so-called 'gift of tongues' I could speak the words at normal volume or very quietly and I could have stopped any time I wished. But I was alone and it was a long time before I chose to stop. The experience was accompanied by a marvellous awareness of the presence and reality of God who had sent Jesus and released the Holy Spirit in Jesus' name. I sensed the limitless spiritual refreshment of which Jesus spoke at the Feast of Feasts.

The particular issue of 'tongues' has caused much perplexity and much controversy. It features in the lives of many ordinary Christians who, having once experienced it, can use it at will in their prayers. It is vital that it be kept in the perspective which the New Testament gives it. It is explicitly mentioned only in the Acts of the Apostles and in Paul's First Letter to the Corinthians. In Luke's account it does accompany some occasions where people were first 'filled with the Spirit' (Acts 10.46, 19.6), while the Pentecost story in Acts 2 offers the specific and rare phenomenon of other people recognising the languages spoken. Paul refers to it as a gift primarily for private prayer which he values and commends (1 Cor. 14.18) but knows that not all Christians have it (1 Cor. 12.30) and in no way makes it a supreme index of the Spirit's presence and activity. Many Christians value it exactly in Paul's terms. Even when used in a

31

'matter of fact' kind of way, unaccompanied by particular emotion, it can express a sense of worship or a sense of appeal to God which is beyond the limits of rational articulation.

It will be quite apparent that this chapter does not focus on my own or anyone else's experience of praying in strange languages. But it does plead that all who believe in the Holy Spirit should pray in a believing way for the Spirit's presence and activity in their own lives and the life of the churches, open to what God wants to give and grateful for results.

In youthful enthusiasm I expected that a single decisive experience of the Spirit would take my life a quantum leap to a level of unabated joy, guaranteed sanctity and marvellous effectiveness in ministry. It didn't. Nor does the New Testament lead us to anticipate that. Emotions fluctuate. Character is shaped at least partly by effort and constant choices. In varying times and circumstances visible success in Christian work may or may not come.

Yet I can also speak positively. I am regularly delighted by the sheer joy of knowing God. I have been able to be obedient in difficult circumstances to things I had to do. There are times when things I said or prayed have been used to help others in ways which were simply not within my own capability. Above all I have understood the New Testament picture of the Church of Christ as a whole body empowered by God's living presence through his Spirit.

The issue of expectancy

The nature and work of God as Trinity is the supreme theme of Christian theology. No exploration of this theme will diminish the sense of mystery. Some may feel an uncertainty as to when we should speak of God present and active, the risen Jesus present and active or the Holy Spirit present and active. The rough answer is that in many instances we do not need to be too concerned to make distinctions. But the New Testament consistently leads us to acknowledge God as the one known to us through his self-revelation in Jesus and through the empowering activity of his Spirit.

The second-century theologian Irenaeus used a simple but meaningful picture when he spoke of the Son and the Spirit as the two hands of God with which he works in the world. This is a picture emphasising some distinctness but also constant co-operative working.[2]

32

The Bible can give impersonal images for particular aspects of the person and work of Jesus, the image of light being just one. So too it offers impersonal images of water, wind and fire with reference to the free-flowing character of the Spirit's work. Yet the character of the Spirit's work is entirely personal. Both in the coming of Jesus and in the activity of the Spirit we are dealing with the personal presence of God.

A writer called Catherine Marshall has recorded how she first began to think seriously and practically about the Holy Spirit during a long period of quietness and comparative solitude enforced by an illness.[3] In the course of ministry and preaching I have sometimes referred to her example because she was not influenced by anyone else's thinking along the same line.

A sense of private curiosity impelled her to write down in a notebook everything that she could find in the New Testament about the promise of the Spirit. This included the assurance that through the work of Jesus the Spirit would be 'poured out on all flesh' (Acts 2.17), in fulfilment of an Old Testament promise but in contrast to many Old Testament records of the Spirit being given to a few specially chosen people. The Spirit would make Jesus' continuing presence and his teachings real to us. The chief hallmark of the Holy Spirit would be power for service and ministry to others. The Spirit would bind together the fellowship of Christ's body on earth, the Church.

Eventually Catherine came to a point where some action on her part seemed indicated. So she made a simple response of speaking to Jesus in prayer and asking for the gift of the Spirit. Then she consciously embarked on a day-to-day life of seeking to be obedient to God and of expecting to see some evidence of her prayer having been heard and answered, whatever that evidence might prove to be. She says that she experienced no waves of emotion or ecstasy. When she had asked herself, 'Can we expect a manifestation of the Spirit?' she had little idea how to answer. She reasoned that since the Spirit was a person then of course he had personality traits and presumably these traits would manifest themselves. How or in what way, she could not guess.

She began to find a distinct change related to her own character. She found herself being schooled in a discipline of not speaking careless or negative or discouraging words. For weeks she was put through a sharp training of opening her mouth to speak and experiencing a check in terms of 'Stop! Don't say it. Close your mouth'. Other experiences followed which she could not have predicted where she found guidance in a variety of circumstances.

Then in the shock of bereavement following the death of her husband in a car-crash, the compulsory exploration of terrible territory she had never been in before, she was grateful that she had already embarked on a closer intimacy of relationship with God through his Spirit.

In setting herself to write her husband's biography, her first ever attempt to write a book, she knew the severe limitations of her own resources and for a while could not seem to order the material rightly. Then it seemed that she found inspirational help. 'Do it this way'.

At a later time she found that she had the gift of praying in tongues, given with no particular fanfare but rather as a divine quartermaster might casually hand out a tool for a job. 'Here. You'll need this'. Later again came her growing awareness of the vast number of comparable personal journeys experienced by people across the world.

That is Catherine Marshall's individual story. But it points to the basic New Testament encouragement that we would receive the Spirit's help through an attitude of asking. Speaking of parents who know who to give good things to their children Jesus says 'How much more will your heavenly Father give the Holy Spirit to those who ask him'. At least that is Luke's version (11.13). Matthew's version is simply that the Father will give good things to those who ask him (7.11). But either way Jesus promises his disciples that on a basis of asking there is resource available for the business of discipleship which is beyond their own resource.

This particular passage of Jesus' teaching addresses two sorts of fear which can affect us when summoned to open ourselves to God's Spirit, the fear that nothing is going to happen or the fear that something will happen and we won't like it. It also contains an encouragement to perseverance because the processes which God is working in us may well take time and patience.

God's Empowering Presence

I like the story which a distinguished New Testament scholar called Gordon Fee tells of his own background in the Assemblies of God and his early familiarity with Pentecostal styles of passion, sometimes very suspicious of academic approaches.[4] One day, in his fourth year of pastoring a church, he walked into his study after lunch and picked

34

up the post. He was glancing through a copy of the magazine 'Christianity Today' when he came across a letter by a fellow minister of his own denomination, attacking the magazine for its intellectual approach to Christianity. The letter concluded with the words, 'I would rather be a fool on fire than a scholar on ice!'

In that moment the Holy Spirit spoke into my heart and I dropped my head on my desk and I wept and wept. The Holy Spirit said, 'There are two other options'. I had seen fools on ice but I had never seen a scholar on fire.

He prayed that if it was possible he might become a scholar on fire. He began to apply himself in an academic direction, even though it was initially far from straightforward. Eventually he became New Testament Professor at Regent College in Vancouver and has been the author of numerous books and commentaries. A book called 'God's Empowering Presence', published in 1994, is a detailed commentary on the numerous passages in the letters of Paul which have some Holy Spirit reference. This is a large book, running to nearly a thousand pages.

The Spirit is not the centre for Paul - Christ is, ever and always - but the Spirit stands very close to the centre, as the crucial ingredient of all genuinely Christian life and experience.[5]

At the conclusion Fee says he has no intention to be judgemental but he see that in much of its subsequent history the Church kept Trinitarian belief more as a matter of theology than experience.[6] Yet he also finds much cause for rejoicing in the Church's history. His plea is for recapturing Paul's perspective of Christian life as essentially the life of the Spirit, dynamically experienced but fully integrated into the life of the Church.

'......let us have the Spirit bring life into our present institutions, theologies, and liturgies. The Spirit not only inspires a new hymnody in every renewal within the church, but makes the best of former hymnodies come to life with new vigour. 'Can these dry bones live?', the Lord asked the prophet. 'You know', he replied, and then watched as the Spirit brought life to what was already there.

In recapturing the life of the Spirit there will be the renewal of particular gifts familiar in the New Testament, not for the sake of being charismatic, but for the building up of the people of God for their life together and in the world. Definitely there must be proper care and discernment as well (1 Thess.5.19). The Church will be more vitally Trinitarian, meaning not the exaltation of the Spirit but the exaltation of God, not focus on the Spirit as such but on Jesus as the crucified and risen Saviour and Lord. The Church will be a joyous community and its life will be 'decidedly over against the world's present trinity of relativism, secularism and materialism with their thoroughly dehumanising effects'. He believes Paul's perspective must become our own if we are going to make any difference at all in the so-called post-Christian era.

> *But this means that our theologising must stop paying mere lip service to the Spirit..... The church must risk freeing the Spirit from being boxed into the creed and getting him back into the life of the believer and the believing community.*

Gordon Fee is not the only New Testament scholar who has wanted to apply Paul's theology of the Spirit directly to the present-day life of the Church. For example, James Dunn in his book 'Jesus and the Spirit' (1975) had said how attracted he was by the vitality and maturity with which Paul expounded the Spirit's work. He said that perhaps here lay the biggest challenge to twentieth-century Christianity:

> *..... to be open to that experience of God which first launched Christianity and to let that experience, properly safeguarded as Paul insisted, create new expressions of faith, worship and mission at both individual and corporate level. One thing we may be sure of: the life of the Christian church can go forward only when each generation is able creatively to interpret its gospel and its common life out of its own experience of the Spirit and word which first called Christianity into existence.*[7]

Whether in the invigoration of what is there already or in creating 'new expressions', the Spirit must be freed from being boxed into the Creed.

An experience of Alpha

Using the Alpha course at a local Methodist Church during the 1990s we followed Alpha's suggested pattern of a special event about halfway through the course which would take as its main subject the work of the Holy Spirit. For this we used a Saturday afternoon in a different location to our normal weeknight meeting-place. We started with a shared lunch and followed a varied programme for the afternoon which ended with a time of quietness giving people space for their own prayers. For those who wished we offered that one or two of us would come and stand with them, put an individual blessing on them and pray simply for the continuing activity of God's Spirit in their lives.

No stress was placed on the expectation of any one particular outcome of this prayer or that they would necessarily feel or experience something definable in the time of praying. Our emphasis was on trusting God to show in his own time and way that he acknowledges our seeking him.

Afterwards a young woman, already a church member, shared privately that in these moments of being prayed for she spontaneously felt the same sense of peaceful excitement that she had felt when she first became a Christian seven years before. A while later I asked her if she would speak in a meeting and say something personal about her own journey in faith. For a short time she struggled with the invitation because her natural response would have been to say that she couldn't do things like that and was just not that sort of person. But she now knew she was meant to do it and she did so. The capacity to talk openly about her faith was a new development in her life. Something in this area had been unlocked.

Not publicly but privately she spoke of a profound increase of love within her marriage. She also displayed a special kind of energy and dedication in helping another couple as they passed through a testing time. It seemed like a particular thing prepared for her to do.

She remained the same person as before. But the changes and developments were distinct and they surprised her. All such changes belong to what the great medieval theologian Thomas Aquinas called the 'innovationes' of the Holy Spirit, the unexpected new things [8].

I am not here pleading on behalf of the Alpha course. The plea is on behalf of the Holy Spirit, for whom fresh spaces need to be found. The Spirit is credited with activating in us the whole effect of Jesus' work, assuring us of God's love for us, helping our understanding, assisting our prayers, shaping our character, impelling us to show God's love to others in word and deed, creating among us varied gifts and styles of service. God loves mutuality within the life of the Church and the prayers which Christians pray for each other are often a means for the release of blessing. This does not discount but reinforces the significance of baptism or confirmation where the individual's profession of faith is accompanied by prayer for the gift of the Spirit. But for many a fully personal discovery of the Spirit's work has come at some later time than their Christian beginnings.

There are those who may want to give a psychological explanation of testimonies to the Holy Spirit's work. The New Testament tells us to be careful in discerning the true activity of the Spirit and sometimes it is not straightforward to distinguish what is really of God and what is mainly human. But God can truly be at work even when there might also be some level of psychological explanation. Our human 'psyche' is responding to the presence of God's Spirit. How is God to work in us if not somehow through the wiring of our brains? How is he to relate to us if not through the way he has made us?

God's Spirit is active in all sorts of ways in a large variety of churches. Yet many churches have an ethos that the life of the Church can be built on a basis of dedicated adherence, reasonable worship, intelligent planning, utilisation of people's gifts, expressions of social concern and attitudes of friendship and inclusiveness. Of course all these things are capable of being deeply inspired by the Spirit of God. Yet they are also things which we may readily feel we can 'manage'. Whereas openness to the Holy Spirit makes us conscious of vital dependence on God for every part of Christian life. It is in the climate of openness to the Spirit that people become constantly aware of God himself as present and active.

On one occasion when I had the opportunity of talking to a group of people about the Holy Spirit I was praying in advance and I distinctly felt God saying:

Tell them to go with the Spirit and not to be afraid. The Spirit leads to proliferation of life, hope of all sorts and God's fresh touch on inherited things.

4. THE LARGE PICTURE

Rain on the roof in Antioch

MY wife and I had a meal together one evening in 1998 on the outskirts of Antakya, which is situated in the south-eastern corner of Turkey not far from the border with Syria. In Roman times this was the location of one of the largest and most significant cities of the Mediterranean world.

The waiter who was serving us spoke good English. Suddenly he said, 'I will make you feel at home'. He went off and a couple of minutes later we heard above us the gentle patter of water. There was a sprinkler system to refresh the profuse greenery that was climbing all over the glass roof. He had switched it on so that the sound of rain might remind us of a typical English summer evening.

We told him that we were part of a Christian group visiting Turkey. We were involved in a project called the 'Reconciliation Walk', expressing sorrow for false views of Christianity projected in the Middle East especially by the violence and atrocities which accompanied the Crusades. The waiter told us that he belonged to the Alawi sect of Islam which gives particular reverence to Jesus.

Towards the end of our meal he came back once more and said, 'I've met some more people like you'. He led us across to another table in the crowded restaurant area. What he meant was that he had found some more Christians. They were Greek Orthodox, a local family with parents and adult children. The father and one of the sons worked together as goldsmiths. They cheerfully invited us to sit down with them. Even though we'd already eaten they ordered an enormous basket of fruit and said, 'Eat, eat!'

We appreciated many aspects of our visit to this city where, according to the Acts of the Apostles, 'the disciples were first called Christians'. For years before the opportunity of being there I had been impressed by the account which Luke gives in the second half of Acts chapter 11. Followers of Jesus, including some of African origin, came on mission to Antioch within a dozen years of Easter. Luke says that 'the hand of the Lord was with them' (Acts 11.21). Their message met with striking response both from within the city's Jewish sector and from members of the cosmopolitan population who had no background in Judaism.

We know that Antioch was distinguished for its thriving commerce, sophisticated technology, sporting pursuits and leisure industry, plus the contemporary mix of religions, philosophies, spiritual aspirations and widespread scepticism. Its inhabitants were also famous for a sharp satirical wit and caustic nicknames sometimes given to prominent persons. It was here that a plain name was given to the growing new community of those who believed that Jesus of Nazareth was the Christ (Greek for 'Messiah'). They were called Christians, 'Christ people' (Acts 11.26).

In this chapter I want to set the contemporary call of God in the light of the large picture of Christian history. I have sometimes offered people an outline of ALL THE CHURCH HISTORY YOU MAYBE EVER WANTED TO KNOW. This fits onto a single sheet of paper and divides the events of two millennia into approximate quarters. Such an account, however sketchy, gives some framework for understanding the emergence of different denominations and the historical setting of some famous 'great Christians'.

- The Roman Empire, which already provided the unified administration of the Mediterranean world by the time of Jesus, endured until the fifth century when it broke up. During this period the Christian Church had moved from being a small minority, spasmodically persecuted, to being the state religion of the Empire (after conversion of the Emperor Constantine in 312). Christianity was present in Roman Britain. To these centuries we owe widespread agreement about which books make up Christian Scripture, about creeds that defined belief in face of many variants and about forms of prayer, worship and ordained ministry.

- Various waves of invasion repeatedly disrupted civilised life in Europe. Also the power of Islam began to spread from about 630 onwards and quickly dominated territories in the Middle East and North Africa which had been outstanding areas of early Christian growth. The Church in the West, based on Rome, gradually drifted apart from the Church in the East, based on Constantinople. Christian faith and mission and scholarship did stay alive, especially thanks to monastic communities with their disciplined way of life. England was re-evangelised by Celtic missions from Ireland via Scotland as well as by initiative from Rome.

40

- From the 11th century greater stability returned and Western civilisation was reborn. Some outstanding Christian thinkers wrestled with large questions of Christian revelation and its relation with reason. This was the period of medieval Christendom and the close linkage of Church and State. The Church was often marked by worldly standards and dubious enterprises (e.g. the Crusades). But there were times and places of fresh inspiration for communicating the message of Jesus, for example with Francis and his followers in 13th century Italy or with John Wycliffe and his preachers in 14th century England.

- In the 16th century the Protestant Reformation reacted against the corruptions of the late medieval church with widespread rediscovery of essential New Testament teaching. In England the Anglican church became shaped by the English Bible (William Tyndale and others) and by the Prayer Book of Thomas Cranmer. Some sought greater freedom from set forms and state control (Presbyterians, Congregationalists, Baptists, Quakers). From the 18th century onwards Christianity was facing strong currents of rationalism questioning its truth. But evangelical revivals, Methodism in particular, had a large impact and missionary movements from Europe created the basis of the 'World Church'. The 20th century brought fresh understanding between Christians of different traditions as well as massive worldwide growth of new churches. It also brought serious decline of Church life in Western Europe, the main centre of its historic strength.

From Easter onwards Christianity lives always between past and future. It is a faith with a historical base in the life, death and resurrection of Jesus of Nazareth and it is a faith with an ongoing story through centuries of human affairs. It invites us to a present relationship with God through Jesus, a spiritual knowledge and intimacy which is not dependent merely on tradition and inherited forms. But we also appreciate how those in previous generations experienced the call of God in their own circumstance and we can often be stimulated by their example. Christians believe that God is at work in history for the constant revitalisation of the Church, so that there can be fresh witness to the truth of Jesus in new generations and across boundaries of language, nationality and culture.

The worst of the past

We need to face Christian history at its worst as well as its best. There is a Latin phrase which is relevant to the many circumstances where Christianity gets corrupted. 'Corruptio optimi pessima'. The worst sort of corruption is the corruption of what is best. Often people have carried the name of Christian with attitudes and behaviour partly or totally at variance with the teaching and example of Christ.

The army of the First Crusade left Cologne in 1096 with the intention of winning Jerusalem back from Muslim occupation. There were costly battles before the army ever reached the Holy Land, including the struggle to capture Antioch which involved a nine-month siege and enormous Crusader casualties. Eventually the Crusaders captured Jerusalem in July 1099 and massacred its Muslim and Jewish inhabitants with appalling brutality.[1]

When my wife and I went to Turkey for three weeks of summer 1998 we were part of an international group of about forty. These were from various European countries and also some from America and New Zealand who reckoned on having European ancestry. Altogether over a three year period between 1996 and 1999 more than two thousand Christians went from the West to the Middle East, for shorter or longer periods of time, as part of a single project. The purpose was to express sorrow for the sins of Christian Europe, especially marking the 900th Anniversary of the First Crusade.

The Turkish term for the Crusader is simply 'man of the cross'. Of course the Crusades are only part of the story of varied historical relationships between Christians and Muslims, including periods of peaceful co-operation and other times of confrontation in which both sides could behave viciously. However, the Crusades did deeply affect Middle Eastern attitudes to Western Christians. They presented a Christianity which was cruel and militaristic, concerned for power, wealth and earthly authority at any cost.

Our own participation in the project gave us great respect for its leader, Lynn Green, and the others who originated it and carried it through. They were convinced that something currently needed to be done in the Middle East which was not aimed at persuading people to change religious allegiance but at demonstrating attitudes of contrition, humility and friendship. The Reconciliation Walk was a symbolic measure designed to increase understanding between Western Christians and Muslims, Jews and Eastern Christians.

When the idea of a prayer walk down the routes of the first Crusade was first proposed to Lynn Green he had not wanted to be diverted from his existing engagements. About six months later he was standing in a swimming pool when, to quote his own words, 'I felt God speak to me about it out of the blue. This has happened to me only a few times in my life. I became absolutely captivated'. He was very moved by the reception which many leaders of religious and secular communities gave to the Reconciliation Walk all the way from Cologne to Jerusalem. In Cologne at Easter 1996 the Imam of a local mosque said, 'Your message thrills me and fills me with hope. This idea must have come from an epiphany. What you are doing gives a model for what we should be doing, because we too have done wrong things in history'.

During the three weeks of 1998 that we were in Turkey ourselves we spent short periods of time in three centres - Istanbul, Cappadocia and Antakya. In all these places the group spent time conversing with people on the streets, carrying the following message in Turkish to explain why we had come.

900 years ago our forefathers carried the name of Jesus Christ in battle across the Middle East. Fueled by fear, greed and hatred, they betrayed the name of Christ by conducting themselves in a manner contrary to his wishes and character. The Crusaders lifted the banner of the Cross above your people. By this act they corrupted its true meaning of reconciliation, forgiveness and selfless love.... Where they were motivated by hatred and prejudice, we offer love and brotherhood. Jesus the Messiah came to give life. Forgive us for allowing his name to be associated with death. Please accept again the true meaning of the Messiah's words. 'The Spirit of the Lord is upon me because has anointed me to bring good news to the poor. He has sent me to proclaim release to the captives and recovery of sight to the blind, to let the oppressed go free, to proclaim the year of the Lord's favour'.

For ourselves it was the first time of being in Istanbul and seeing one of the mightiest Christian churches ever built, Ayia Sophia (Holy Wisdom), which stands directly opposite an enormous mosque. This city of Constantinople was the centre of a Christian Empire for a thousand years but with its capture by the Turks in 1453 became the centre of a great Muslim Empire. In fact the church of Ayia Sophia

43

was ringed around with seven mosques as if to say 'We'll show you power!'. Christianity with all its trappings of political and military might as well as its massive works of architecture had not helped Muslims to see the essence of following the way of Jesus.

In Antakya my wife and I met a teenage girl who told us simply that the message was worth a million dollars. We met policemen who spontaneously said they must also reflect on what their own nation had done. We went to one of the mosques where two elderly officials considered the message quietly and respectfully, then took us down to a crypt to see some early Christian burials. In another mosque members of our group met an Imam who did seek to engage them in a dialogue about faith by asking 'Why can you not believe that Muhammad is the Seal of the Prophets?'

In my own mind there is no compromise of Christian belief in the uniqueness of Jesus. I know that Muhammad brought to the Arabian tribes a sincere form of monotheistic devotion. But those who have come to know God in a New Testament light cannot then consider that Muhammad is truly the Seal of the Prophets. There are appropriate times and places where those of different faiths can share their convictions with complete honesty. But wherever faith in Jesus is proclaimed it must be with visible demonstration of the attitudes prescribed by Jesus in the Sermon on the Mount.

Since the Reconciliation Walk finished in Jerusalem in the summer of 1999 some who were involved have stayed in the Middle East, seeking to continue a contribution to reconciliation especially in the land of Israel.

Another sketch of history

In chapter 13 of Mark's Gospel Jesus tells his followers what they are to expect from the future. This is part of Mark's account of the final days of Jesus' ministry and the location is the Mount of Olives, with a view of the architecturally magnificent new Temple which forty years later the Romans destroyed. Jesus outlines some characteristics of future history, however long that history may prove to be.

- There will be deceptions. False claimants to the authority which properly belongs to Jesus will lead many people astray. (We can understand this with reference to the Messianic pretenders who repeatedly arose in Israel's continuing history, but also with reference to other leaders in many times and places who have claimed excessive authority).

- There will be disasters both of human and natural agency in wars, earthquakes and famines. (In a physical universe we remain vulnerable to physical forces and with no guarantees of security. Suffering is constantly increased and exacerbated by the effects of human sinfulness.)

- There will be persecution of Jesus' followers involving interrogations, punishments and executions. Facing his own impending death Jesus tells the disciples not to be surprised by the manifestations of hatred which they will meet later.

The forecast does not mean that Christians can be complacent when these things occur. Christians must be vitally concerned with challenging deception, preventing and alleviating suffering, coming to the help of the persecuted. But Jesus is saying that his followers' faith in him is not to be shaken. Belief in him includes believing him when he tell us to anticipate these things. From the first century AD to the twenty-first the predictions of Jesus are graphically illustrated.

This account might seem drastically negative in its neglect of future cultural achievement or scientific progress or opportunities of human enjoyment. But Christianity vitally unites the grateful appreciation of human life and its rich possibilities with the realistic recognition of suffering and loss. This unity is seen supremely in Jesus himself. In Mark 13 the primary issue is preparation for the hard situations in which much of Christian experience will have to be lived out.

Part of the chapter relates specifically to the destruction of Jerusalem in AD70 while another part presents an ultimate horizon to history, expressed in strongly apocalyptic imagery. As usual the main thrust of the New Testament witness is not speculation about the conclusion of history but the call to live in constant accountability to God in the light of eternity.

Some scholars have reckoned that only a limited amount of this chapter really goes back to Jesus himself and that Mark here brings together elements from a variety of sources, such as prophetic utterances from within the early Christian community. There is no sufficient reason to think that Mark ever constructed his material so freely.[2] But it is certainly possible that sayings of Jesus on various occasions have been combined in a single dramatic context.

In its sombre surroundings verse 10 stands out strongly. 'The good news must first be proclaimed to all nations'. Here is Mark's setting for an instruction corresponding to the Great Commission in Matthew. Already by the time Mark's Gospel was written, some thirty years after Easter, there were Christian communities established in many parts of the Roman world. A network of house-churches was well established in Rome itself and Christians became the target of a cruel persecution under the Emperor Nero. But for all the subsequent centuries the imperative remains that the message of Jesus should be offered universally and its truth lived out in face of all challenges.

Jesus characteristically spoke of the 'Kingdom of God' as having decisively arrived in him and in his ministry. This central demonstration of God's sovereign presence and activity culminated in Jesus' death and resurrection. For as long as history lasts there is to be the dynamic continuation of Jesus' ministry and constant signs of the Kingdom.

A book called 'Miracle in Mostar' describes the growth of a particular Christian community in a Bosnian city during the turmoil of the 1990s. This church lovingly incorporated people from varied ethnic backgrounds. It was marked by outstanding courage and prayerfulness, sensitive witness to the transforming power of Jesus and dedicated practical outreach in care and comfort. Sometimes worship and bible teaching would be going on in an apartment building to the sound of gunfire in the city around. At these times the leaders gently discouraged newcomers from looking out of the window to see what was going on. 'They have their business to do and we have ours'.[3]

The story of Patrick

In the current situation of the decline of organised Christianity in Britain many have found renewed inspiration in the Celtic period, finding a link between our own era and that much earlier time when faith made its way after the collapse of the Christianised Roman Empire. The Celtic name is given to forms of Christianity which belonged in Ireland, Scotland, Wales and Cornwall but had missionary influence across England and into Europe. Its most fertile time was about 400 to 700 AD but its effects did continue a lot longer. Its most famous names are perhaps Patrick of Ireland, Columba of Iona, Aidan and Hilda and Cuthbert in Northumbria, although it embraces the lives and adventures of numerous others.

These are some of the familiar threads of Celtic Christianity:

- a profound sense of God's love in Jesus Christ;

- an emphasis on holiness of character and uncompromising discipleship;

- a gentle and attractive approach to others in their own idiom and building bridges into their experience;

- a deep love of nature and its revelation of God, while balancing the sense of 'God in everything' with God's transcendence as well and specific revelation in Jesus;

- a spirit of artistic creativity;

- the experience of the miraculous, especially demonstrations in Jesus' name against the power of evil and the occult;

- a strong missionary impulse and acceptance of any hardship in this cause;

- a care for practical and social need and compassion for the poor.

Celtic Christianity emphasised the Trinity. Trinitarian teaching gave a structure to their understanding of God, to their profound prayer life and to their living out of a passionate Christian calling. It is frequently reflected in the balanced rhythms of ancient Celtic poetry as well as in modern prayers in a Celtic idiom.

Patrick is known for his extraordinary achievement in converting a pagan nation to Christianity, the beginning of a period of history in which Ireland was a remarkable centre of Christian influence. I was most impressed when I first discovered that in Patrick's so-called 'Confession' we possess the autobiographical account of his early experiences. Primary to all other accounts and the encrustations of legend the voice of this passionate fifth-century missionary still speaks to us directly.

Patrick describes his capture by pirates when he was a teenager and his several years of servitude in Ireland looking after animals. He discovered intimacy with God in the years of his late teens through the circumstances of his own disaster, finding a large appetite for prayer in open-air solitude in Irish fields and woods. He recounts the miraculous sense of guidance which led him in his eventual escape, the laborious journey via the Continent until he was reunited with his parents in England, his desire never to return to the place from which he had escaped with such difficulty and the promptings in dreams and visions which finally impelled him to do so. The account does become limited in regard to the actual missionary work in Ireland and has little detail of the many years of journeys and encounters. But there is an overall tone of amazement that somehow under God's hand his mission turned out in an exceptional way. He has a genuine modesty in his own sense of ordinariness.

The story of Patrick using a shamrock leaf as a visual aid for the Trinity is only legendary. But his personal testimony illuminates his Trinitarian faith. Under the title 'Aristocracy of Soul' Noel O'Donoghue has written a commentary on the 'Confession'.[4] Here three successive chapters are headed 'The Experience of God the Father', 'The Discovery of Jesus Christ' and 'The Fellowship of the Holy Spirit'.

- Patrick's separation from a human father became a living encounter with the Fatherhood of God. He encountered a consoling and liberating love in a time of loneliness and extremity. He sees the Father in relation to his own boyhood, in a childlike relationship that remains full of wonder and gratitude.

- The road that leads to the Father becomes also the road leading to the discovery of the Son in the face of Jesus Christ, God and man. Especially for Patrick there is a realisation and exploration of his vital union with the poverty and suffering of Jesus. The fears and hardships of the missionary life which are his daily companions are not to be seen as unfortunate or disabling; they were the companions of Jesus Christ himself.

- Patrick also speaks repeatedly about awareness of the Holy Spirit as a presence within the depths of his own spirit. If the Father is above him and Jesus Christ is beside him, the Holy Spirit is within him. At a dramatic point in his story it was consciousness of the Spirit through his dreams which prompted the return of Patrick to Ireland. But the Spirit remains also a continuing reality of his experience. 'The Spirit within his spirit binds Patrick to his mission as well as assuring him of support and consolation'.[5]

The old Irish prayer traditionally called 'Patrick's Breastplate' is probably not from Patrick himself but certainly expresses his conviction.

> *I arise today*
> *Through a mighty strength, the invocation of the Trinity,*
> *Through belief in the threeness,*
> *Through confession of the oneness*
> *Of the Creator of the Creation.....*

I will let these words stand in their own right as the climax of this chapter, because Christian history is the large picture of all those who in huge variety of place and circumstance have found their strength in the invocation of the Trinity. The next chapters consider two particular movements, Methodism which began in the eighteenth century and Pentecostalism in the twentieth. In both cases what happened in the past is relevant for the present.

5.   GOD AND METHODISM

Some genuine history

In 1988 British Methodism celebrated 250 years since John Wesley's 'heart-warming', a key event in Methodism's memory of its origins. At that time I was stationed in the village of Tuxford in Nottinghamshire. The Chapel planned a local celebration which would also recall the 200 years since John Wesley had preached in Tuxford. I didn't possess a copy of Wesley's Journal but from a library someone had produced a photocopy of the Journal entry for July 3rd 1788.

> *I was going to preach in Tuxford, near the end of the town; but the gentry sent and desired me to preach in the market-place; which I accordingly did, to a large and attentive congregation, on 'It is appointed unto men once to die'.*

On the afternoon of Sunday July 3rd 1988 a local Methodist, suitably dressed for the part, came on a horse into the village market-place. He was much more youthful than the Wesley of 1788, who would have been in his mid-eighties and travelling by carriage rather than on horseback. But we opted for the popular image. The gathered crowd moved from the market-place to the more convenient space of a large playing-field and we held an open air service, not addressed by the horse-rider but by a visiting speaker from Nottingham. People reckoned it had been a good afternoon and photos stayed on display in Chapel for many months.

A year later, shortly to leave the area, I was in someone's house where I noticed Wesley's Journal on the shelves. Looking up 3rd July 1788 I was surprised to find the words 'I was going to preach in Alford', plus a footnote to the effect that one copy of the journal had 'Tuxford' in error. Alford is a place in Lincolnshire, which made much better sense in the context of other Lincolnshire names before and after. So we had not only altered Wesley's age and mode of transport but had celebrated something which never happened at all. I kept this new information to myself. At least the Journal shows that Wesley stopped for a cup of tea in Tuxford on a Saturday afternoon in June 1786 while travelling northwards by carriage from Newark.

Methodism is an outstanding example of a dramatic Christian movement which grew into a major worldwide Church. Its history is of interest to many who are not Methodists themselves.

Lincolnshire is the county of John Wesley's own origins, where he and his brother Charles grew up in the Rectory at Epworth as part of a large family.   Both of them became students at Oxford University and John went on to become a Fellow of Lincoln College. In the early 1730s a small group of students met regularly for Bible study and prayer, received Communion frequently and undertook works of charity.   Their methodical and devout lifestyle attracted attention and some ridicule. Various nicknames were given including the 'Holy Club' and a name which proved enduring, 'the Methodists'. Another member of this group was George Whitefield who within a few years had become a well-known preacher outstanding for his oratorical gifts.

John and Charles became ordained clergymen of the Church of England and both responded to an invitation to serve as chaplains in British colonial settlements in America. This was a period of considerable difficulty and disillusionment for them but they were specially impressed by the qualities of faith and character which they found in German Christians from the so-called Moravian community. When they were back in London in 1738 both brothers had regular conversations with a German called Peter Boehler to whom Charles was giving English lessons.

Boehler believed that John and Charles were still struggling along on the basis of their own sincerity. They had not yet found 'faith' in its true New Testament sense, a relationship with God based purely on his initiative of love towards us in Jesus. 'Justification by faith alone' was the heart of Martin Luther's experience and teaching and the mainspring of the sixteenth century Protestant Reformation. In one conversation in February 1738, when Charles said he hoped for salvation because he had used his best endeavours to serve God, Boehler shook his head and said no more. Charles thought him very uncharitable.[1] But both brothers were wrestling with a new possibility.   During April and into May they were reading the New Testament avidly and reading Martin Luther as well.

On Whitsunday May 21st Charles found a transforming sense of peace and assurance. Then when he opened his Bible the first words to which his eye came were from Psalm 40, 'He has put a new song in my mouth.' On May 23rd he composed a hymn, 'Where shall my

52

wondering soul begin?', which was the first of an extraordinary output of hymns throughout the remainder of his life. On the evening of May 24th at a prayer meeting in Aldersgate Street, while someone was reading from the writings of Luther, John felt his heart 'strangely warmed'. 'I felt I did trust in Christ, Christ alone, for salvation; and an assurance was given me that he had taken away my sin, even mine, and rescued me from the law of sin and death'.[2] Afterwards he would characteristically say that up to that time he had 'the faith of a servant' but now he had 'the faith of a son'.

In 1739 both brothers followed the example of George Whitefield and took the radical step of starting to preach in the open air. Their enthusiastic preaching had already made them unwelcome in many churches and in any case the outdoor preaching gave the opportunity of addressing large numbers who had little contact with the life of the Church. They began to see the effects of the preaching in many hundreds of people who turned to God in a heartfelt way and found their own experiences of total renewal.

Wesley developed pastoral organisation by which local Methodist societies were also divided into small groups known as 'classes', meeting weekly for fellowship and encouragement. The leadership gifts of lay people were allowed full expression. There was a gradual process of chapel building as local societies felt the need of their own places to meet and worship. It was the intention that Methodism would remain within the Church of England and that Methodists would attend their parish churches as well as Methodist meetings. But increasingly the overall strength and cohesion of the movement, and its discrepancy from the formalism of much of the contemporary Anglican scene, resulted in separation. This process was accelerated in 1784 by John Wesley's ordination of his own ministers for the needs of developing Methodist work in America.

The movement became well-known, though its initial numerical strength should not be exaggerated. In 1775, thirty-five years after the Wesleys began preaching in the open air, the members of Methodist societies numbered 30,000 in a total population of about 10 million.[3] But there was considerable further growth during the next forty years as well as fresh signs of renewal in the Anglican Church and elsewhere. The evangelical revival represented by Methodism but also by other streams was at the heart of the modern missionary movement and also some remarkable pieces of social engagement, notably the patient but ultimately successful campaign for the abolition of slavery.

The story of Methodism's worldwide growth and influence over two centuries is vast and varied.[4] By the year 2000 membership figures were about 30 million. There is continuing increase in numerical strength as gains in Africa, Asia and Latin America outweigh losses in Britain and North America.

Methodist character

Reading about ordinary eighteenth-century Methodists whose names may be unfamiliar still helps us to understand the nature of the movement. Here are just two examples.[5] As it happens there are common features between these two in their Yorkshire setting and in the part which bereavement played in intensifying their spiritual search. But their records are typical of many others and without any standard profile of previous life-experience.

Henry Longden was born in Sheffield in 1754 and at the age of 15 became a razor-maker's apprentice. In his late teens he was drinking hard and fighting hard. After a particular Sunday when he and a few others had drunk a huge quantity of gin he was brought home insensible and was ill for weeks. Then his father's death had a major impact. 'I was an enigma to myself. I felt in my soul a painful void'. He went to a Methodist Chapel and was immediately impressed by the simple directness of the preacher's prayers and address and by the beautiful character of the congregational singing. 'In the fullness of my heart I said, This people shall be my people and their God shall be my God for ever'.

He joined a class and continued uncertainly for a time, troubled that so much of his life had been 'an act of daring contempt' against God. Not finding his way out from the sense of painful struggle he was told by his class leader that he was putting too much trust in his own attempts at repentance, his own sorrow, his own spiritual effort, 'instead of pleading in faith the death and mediation of Jesus Christ'. By this advice he came finally into a sense of joy and peace he had not known before, with an ongoing longing that his life might express Christian character perfectly. He was specially impressed by Paul's words in 1 Thessalonians, 'May the God of peace sanctify you wholly' (5.23).

With hesitancy he accepted for himself the role of class leader, which he considered 'by far the most important office among the Methodists', and he gained an experience of leadership which was later applied in his supervision of class-leaders over a wide area. He was clearly a person of profound qualities. Not untypically for his time he had rather severe views on the proper upbringing of children but it appears that these mellowed considerably.

The second example is Sarah Bentley, who was born in 1767 near Harrogate. She had a very elementary education and from the age of 15 worked as a maid mainly in inns. Her mother during serious illness declared that she would like to see Mr. Dawson of York, who was an elderly man with a reputation as a Methodist preacher. Sarah tried to borrow a horse but got the reply, 'If the parson won't do for her she can have nobody'. So she walked and ran the seven miles to the city to fetch William Dawson. Day after day he rode over regularly to see her mother until her death. Sarah was aware of her mother dying in a calm spirit as a believing Christian.

She went to live at the 'George Inn' in York and worked in the bar. She was now engaged in her own spiritual search and at night she read her Bible in the attic. Friends wanted to encourage her to be sociable and she spent a hard-earned £10 on a dress for a dance. But she was not satisfied by dancing. On Christmas Eve she joined others in a 'large upper room' where a preacher by the name of Richard Burdsall was speaking on the text 'no room in the inn'. She went back again to her attic to pray and had a decisive sense of opening her heart to God's love. Afterwards she told her friends about it, who feared that she really had gone mad.

This was the beginning of a Christian life in which her own understanding and character progressively developed. She deeply influenced others through her teaching of children and her personal example of love and service. When cholera swept through York she nursed the dying. When a wealthy local Countess felt desperate need of spiritual guidance she sent for Sarah and talked with her for about five hours, until 'she obtained that which her soul desired, the assurance of God's forgiving love'.

These biographical instances illustrate Wesley's constant combined emphasis on faith as an unmerited gift from God (justification) and the maturing of Christian character (sanctification). They illustrate passion across the full range of Christian calling:

- Ministry to God: Worship
- Ministry to Believers: Nurture
- Ministry to the World : Evangelism and Mercy

Already in 1742 Wesley had written his own short outline of 'The Character of a Methodist'. He makes clear that he uses the name as one which other people first imposed on his Oxford group. 'I should rejoice (so little ambitious am I to be the head of any sect or party) if the very name might never be mentioned more, but be buried in eternal oblivion'. But if the name was to be used then he wanted to define it.

First he says what the distinguishing marks of a Methodist are not.

- They are not opinions of any sort. 'His assenting to this or that scheme of religion, his embracing any particular set of notions, his espousing the judgement of one man or another, are all quite wide of the point'.
- They are not particular forms of expression. Methodists prefer the most easy and natural words by which a meaning can be conveyed 'both on ordinary occasions and when we speak of the things of God'.
- They are not particular actions or customs in either requiring or forbidding anything except what is covered by the plain meaning of Scripture.
- It is not 'laying the whole stress of religion on any single part of it'. It is a comprehensive understanding of living faith leading to 'holiness of heart and life'.

Positively Wesley's marks of a Methodist include:

- According to the commandments of Jesus they love the Lord their God with all their heart, soul, mind and strength'.
- They have contentment in all circumstances, knowing how to accept blessings with gratitude and deprivations without complaining.
- They have a constant practice of prayer, both in times specially set aside for prayer but also as an underlying attitude in the normal business of life.
- They show love to others, according to Jesus' commands, showing active care for neighbours and goodwill even to enemies.
- They have purity of heart and a comprehensive desire to please God in everything.

Wesley intends to define Methodism in terms of fundamental New Testament Christianity. 'From real Christians, of whatever denomination they be, we earnestly desire not to be distinguished at all'.

Assurance then and now

In spite of challenge and ridicule both from within and outside churches Methodism encouraged the expectation that there would be a felt evidence of God's accepting and pardoning love. A classic text for the so-called 'doctrine of assurance' is Romans 8.16, where Paul speaks of a joyful and intimate knowledge of God's Fatherhood mediated through Jesus. 'The Spirit bears witness with our spirit that we are children of God'. John Wesley and his preachers did discuss whether they were anticipating too much uniformity and whether the pressure for certainty was driving some into despair. Gradually John became more open to variation in the way that the Holy Spirit worked in different people, not insisting that being a recipient of God's grace meant having had a special assurance of it. But he did not reject the importance of assurance itself as something which Christians would hope for. [6]

Certainly by the second half of the twentieth century there were those in Methodism who strongly expressed a view that Wesleyan doctrine was inadequate for the current age. As a University student I was impressed by the general stance of John Vincent's book 'Christ and Methodism'.[7] It was one of the influences which kept me on track of wanting to enter the ministry. It presented applications of the Gospel story in terms of radical commitment to addressing social need. But it did also attempt to debunk evangelical teaching to the point of saying that justification by faith was 'gobbledygook' for modern hearers.

A book called 'Towards a Radical Church', written by Richard Jones and Anthony Wesson and published in 1970, also sought a spirituality which would first frankly acknowledge that many modern Methodists simply could not speak of experiences like those recorded from early Methodism.

It has normally been assumed that central Christian experience is the awareness that one is a sinful, unworthy, undeserving mortal with no right whatever to the goodness of God; that one meets up with the overwhelming wonder of the love, forgiveness and acceptance of Christ, vows one's total allegiance to him, confesses faith in him, is converted and then lives intimately in union with him.... All this is in chaos at present. The modern Christian simply does not receive an experience which tallies with this sort of map.[8]

The authors stated and then explored their own view. 'Christian experience is primarily that of seeing the truth about the whole of life, discovering that it is demonstrated to us in Jesus Christ and knowing that one must commit oneself to him'. This is a conviction, a 'whole cast of mind and being on which one is prepared to act and live', without needing or striving for a supposed revelation of special certainty.

I know that we must be careful of people prescribing, whether for others or for themselves, in exactly what way they want God to reveal himself. I am not arguing against commitments to Jesus experienced as a 'whole cast of mind and being'. Far from it! But we have ventured too far in discounting experiences which the New Testament clearly endorses. So I will quote a few more of the observations that were made in 1970 by 'Towards a Radical Church', because similar sentiments have affected many in Methodism.[9]

- It is suggested that traditional teaching is too morbid and assumes that a sense of sin is the beginning of Christian experience. 'Jesus' characteristic preaching is not a castigation of sinners building on a sense of guilt or an exaggerated portrayal of human depravity or a scarifying description of God's wrath'. Rather it is 'news of real life with God available here and now'. It is easy to appreciate what is being said here. But it was the 'news of real life with God available here and now' which was the essential appeal of the Gospel to many people in the eighteenth century, as to Henry Longden when he first encountered Methodist worship. This man did believe he had shown daring contempt of God. But there is no indication that Sarah Bentley was conscious of special sinfulness when she fully opened her heart to God's love. For many in early Methodism and today the forgiveness of sins is a very significant aspect of this certainty but it remains only one aspect.

- Traditional doctrine is viewed as too self-centred and self-obsessed. 'If I am riddled with anxiety about the state of my own soul, I have not yet begun the religious experience of meeting with Christ.... There is merely the glorious freedom now of living with Christ and for him and nothing else about myself really matters'. Yes, it is right to have caution about the dangers of self-centredness or too much introspection. But people have often had journeys of their own to travel before entering that real 'freedom of living with Christ' and finding their energies freshly released in love and service to others.

- Traditional doctrine is regarded as reflecting an atomistic view of human beings which is itself not biblical but far more a reflection of the individualism of the 18th and 19th centuries. 'Man is not an isolated soul whose dealings with God come through one special channel straight from the Father'. But this apparent refusal of an individual view just has to be contrasted with the New Testament insistence on God's loving regard for individual lives, however essential the role of community.

- Traditional doctrine is said to rely too heavily on one major biblical illustration, that of Paul, 'the intense Pharisee with his background of strict obedience to the law, for whom the relief was immeasurable when he found he could be right with God without it'. But Paul certainly did not understand the detail of his own experience as determinative for all whom he led to faith, considering that he was supremely the Apostle to the Gentiles, the whole world outside of Judaism. It is relevant for people of all backgrounds and centuries that we can have a loving relationship with God which is not based first of all on our own standards of attainment. And can we read the Gospel of John or the First Letter of Peter or the 'first commandment' of Jesus himself and seriously say that an emphasis on assurance is too dependent on Paul's peculiar background?

- It is claimed that whenever there is a quest for 'ultimate certainty' the nature of faith becomes distorted. 'Assurance is denied to the Christian. There is no secret revelation of special certainty by which we have no more doubts'. It is true that feelings of certainty

59

can be experienced by people of all religions and none and are not in themselves an argument for truth. Christians have reasons for believing that Jesus is the unique revelation of God and are not guided only by feeling. But those of the first Christian generation did express a felt certainty about the knowledge of God through Jesus even when others thought them mad or dangerous. In the New Testament there is no discrepancy between faith and certainty. Faith is simply the active grasp of what Jesus has made possible. Of course we do not maintain that therefore true Christians will never experience conflicts and questionings and minor or major periods of doubt or depression. Paul gives his own testimony to such experiences (eg. 2 Cor. 1.8-11). The Moravians, so significant in the Wesleyan story, did tend to overdo their claim that real faith would resolve all negative emotions and John Wesley came to realise this.[10]

World Methodism today is greatly varied in its theological emphases. There has been plenty of debate about the significance of John and Charles Wesley for Methodism's contemporary life, whether they are still our vital guides or at least an important major influence or whether their eighteenth-century context and their own attitudes within it are now largely irrelevant. Inevitably this has been linked with larger debates about how far the New Testament itself needs re-interpreting.

I would personally be happy that we never celebrated any more special anniversaries of John or Charles, whether their births, deaths or heart-experiences. But whatever the changes between then and now, I see the essence of their enterprise as still directly relevant.

- Personal encounter with the living God and surrender to his purposes. (One expression of this is in the prayers of the Covenant Service which Methodists were encouraged to observe annually. 'We engage ourselves, for love of Thee, to seek and do Thy perfect will').

- Pursuing the passionate mission of Jesus in the restoration of relationship between needy individuals and a loving God, the building of committed discipleship, the practical expression of love to all humanity without reservation.

60

- Recognition of the dynamic activity of the Holy Spirit as God's own empowering presence in the development of Christian life and character.

God loves Methodism

Like other mainstream denominations British Methodism considerably declined during the second half of the twentieth century in the number of its members, adherents and churches. This has raised serious questions for the future. In the summer of 2004 our representative governing body, the Methodist Conference, approved an important report reviewing the present situation and spelling out the priorities that the Methodist Church would pursue over the next few years, in partnership with others wherever possible.[11] (In the continuing development of ecumenical relationships we now have a specific agreement with the Church of England to work together at overcoming the final remaining obstacles on the way to full visible unity).[12]

The Priorities Report explores and endorses a set of aims which it summarises as follows:

- underpinning everything we do with God-centred worship and prayer
- supporting community development and action for justice, especially among the most deprived and poor - in Britain and worldwide
- developing new confidence in evangelism and in the capacity to speak of God and faith in meaningful ways
- encouraging fresh ways of being Church
- nurturing a culture in the Church which is people-centred and flexible

In the spring of 2004 I had begun to think afresh about British Methodism. I had already had impressions of what God was saying about his overall will for the life of churches. But now a message about Methodism came unexpectedly in my prayers, simple and perfectly distinct. It was that the Methodist Church still constitutes a people in God's sight, that he loves and cares for this people and that in the present time he is calling to them afresh.

Over many years the experience of finding God's presence and activity in many different church settings had made me set very little store by denomination at all. The upshot was that I viewed the local situations where I was stationed as places where I would try to serve the good of Christ's Church. But even as a born and bred Methodist I was not specially interested in the larger denominational edifice or specially fond of Methodist ways of doing things.

I believe in Christian unity no less than before. I have not begun to suppose that somehow Methodism is God's favourite denomination. But I have sensed how he addresses this particular people whom he remembers raising up.

Everything which God speaks to Methodism he prefaces with the words 'I love you'. He does not call to Methodism out of hostility but calls out of pure love towards a people whom he raised up. He calls to us as people whom he lovingly keeps within his purpose. He is intent on claiming those who already belong to him.

He calls us to a high and holy calling to proclaim his name in this generation with all the resources at our disposal - this is like the human capacity of our resource raised to an 'nth' degree by the injection of God's Spirit and being conscious co-workers in his purpose.

He knows the ways that we have dishonoured him and sometimes lost practically all trace of the original marks of Methodist zeal. His intention for us is still to be a people marked by zeal. He calls to us that we should ourselves keep calling out to him saying, 'Lord, where is the zeal, purity, vision and purpose in a people raised up to know you and be known by you?'

I have no intention of offering a different orientation from the one which the Priorities Report already gives when it calls for everything to be underpinned with worship and prayer. But I underline how searching are the tones of divine love, remembrance and intention.

Early Methodism was familiar with experiences of 'wrestling with God', reminiscent of the mysterious story of Jacob in Genesis 32. There are those in Methodism today who are genuinely under God's call but still need to wrestle for a renewed view of the one who has called them.

God brings them to a place where they cry out because the struggle is so intense that they don't want it to go on, but they don't want him to leave either.

One time in praying I felt that God was speaking to Methodist theologians in an encouraging way, drawing them forward on a path of closer engagement with himself, raising the capacity of those who have thought and written at one level to think and write at another level.

Even after the long depletion of its visible strength, and with difficult readjustments still ahead, God is able to bless this denomination and make it a means of blessing to others. This is not a question of sentimental human attachment to the past. It is an intimation of something God wants to do that has a place within the much larger picture of his purposes. I know there are others in British Methodism whose experience has led them to a similar expectancy. But I am not here speaking on behalf of others, simply sharing what has come to me.

I do not presume to know how this will work out. But I encourage people in Methodism, individually and corporately, to tell God that we want to seek him, above and beyond the insistence of any of our own preferences, prejudices and plans. Let no one resent being asked to pray, 'Lord, where is the zeal, purity, vision and purpose....?' There is no implication that we lack all evidence of them. But still it is God alone who fully knows what he wants to do with us. Against the background of our own history we must pray, 'Lord, what you want to find in us, create in us, because you are our God and we are your people'.

6. REMEMBERING THE TWENTIETH CENTURY

Getting hold of the bell-rope

A SWISS pastor called Karl Barth became the most outstanding theologian of the twentieth century. I indulge my own respect for him by bringing him in here. He powerfully expounded the New Testament revelation of the transcendent God in the man Jesus of Nazareth. I love the combination of his massive theological output with the strength of his central conviction. In 1962, when asked for a summary of his thought, he responded with the words of a children's hymn, 'Jesus loves me, this I know, for the Bible tells me so'.

The crisis in European culture and society brought about by the First World War was the context of Barth's commentary on Paul's Epistle to the Romans, first published in 1919. He had written it alongside his pastoral and preaching duties in a church at Safenwil in the Swiss Alps. He believed that the tendencies of nineteenth-century liberalism were to study man's religion rather than God's revelation and so to present Christianity as the highest achievement of the religious search. Instead he emphasised God's transcendence and the total dependence of human beings on God's self-disclosure in Jesus.

This book 'landed like a bombshell in the playground of the theologians', as one Roman Catholic put it. A different image came to Barth's mind:

As I look back upon my course, I seem to myself as one who, ascending the dark staircase of a church tower and trying to steady himself, reached for the banister but got hold of the bell-rope instead. To his horror, he had then to listen to what the great bell had sounded over him, and not over him alone.[1]

The great bell sounded over any attempt to diffuse Christianity into an expression of religious feeling or a programme of human good intentions. 'One cannot speak of God simply by speaking of man in a loud voice'.[2]

Later, between 1932 and 1946, he was to describe his theological understanding with astonishing length and thoroughness in the twelve volumes of his 'Church Dogmatics', including extensive discussions even in the small print of footnotes and excurseses.

65

Someone has described the travellers in this massive terrain as reporting back in the terms of the old Westerns, that there is gold in 'them thar hills'.[3]

There are vital aspects of twentieth-century Christian history which I am not attempting to describe in detail. These include:

- the co-operation between churches which gathered momentum between the World Missionary Conference at Edinburgh in 1910 and the formation of the World Council of Churches in 1948;

- the resistance of the so-called Confessing Church to the policies of Hitler in Nazi Germany, as well as the fortitude in suffering and martyrdom shown by countless Christians under atheistic Communist regimes;

- the stirrings in the Roman Catholic Church in the 1960s through the papacy of John XXIII and the Second Vatican Council;

- the crucial importance of Christian influence in campaigns for racial justice in the United States and in South Africa.

Barth himself played a leading part in the 1930s in voicing the concerns of the Confessing Church. He was also a speaker at the first assembly of the World Council of Churches in Amsterdam in 1948. Towards the end of his life he took a lively interest in the proceedings of the Second Vatican Council, amazed at the transformation visible in the Catholic Church at that juncture. Nor did he cease to emphasise the political and social challenge of the Gospel, forcefully concerned for the pursuit of peace and justice and for the critical prophetic role of the Church against nationalism and imperialism.

In whatever ways other Christian thinkers have reacted to Barth's positions or developed their own directions, he has remained a major influence. In later life he was tending to modify his total rejection of 'natural theology', the knowledge of God dependent on human reason and the observation of creation. He knows there can be all sorts of 'revelations' by which human beings 'may be illumined here and convinced there and overpowered somewhere else....' The world 'could not be God's *creature* and the area of our existence appointed to us by God, if it were not full of revelations. The philosophers and the poets, the musicians and the prophets of all times are aware of it'. But still Christianity is centred on the unique and compelling self-giving of God himself in the man Jesus. 'Everything must be understood against this background. Less than this God did not will to do for us'. [4]

Barth's theology is deeply Trinitarian. According to the Scripture it is God who reveals himself. He reveals himself by existing among us as God. The result is God with us and in us.

Although Barth stands in no direct relation to the emergence of Pentecostalism it is interesting to see his own stress on the Spirit as one whom the Church knows or should know through its experience rather than through theorising.

To have inner ears for the Word of Christ, to become thankful for his work and at the same time responsible for the message about him and, lastly, to take confidence in men for Christ's sake - that is the freedom which we obtain, when Christ breathes on us, when he sends us his Holy Spirit. It is a tremendously big thing and by no means a matter of course to obtain this freedom.[5]

Only where the Spirit is sighed, cried and prayed for, does he become present and newly active. [6]

Azusa Street and after

The Pentecostal and charismatic movements which began in the twentieth century continue strongly into the twenty-first. In these movements the Spirit of God has certainly been sighed, cried and prayed for and has become present and newly active in the lives of large numbers of people.

The Pentecostal movement presented the Gospel in an evangelical way and also stressed the importance of 'baptism in the spirit', as promised by John the Baptist and fulfilled in the experience of Jesus' first followers at Pentecost. This was taught as a specific experience of empowering for Christian life and mission. It was specially associated with the phenomenon of praying in tongues and was linked with expectation of other gifts like prophecy and healing which also feature in the New Testament. These gifts ('charismata' in Greek) also provided a name for the 'charismatic renewal', an informal, international movement within the mainstream churches, beginning in the 1950s and gathering momentum in the 1960s. Many who were affected by this movement began to form their own networks and structures.

Where Methodism looks back to Wesley's 'heart-warming' in 1738, so Pentecostalism looks back to a spontaneous revival which began in 1906.[7] The leader of the Azusa Street revival was a black pastor called Bill Seymour, son of former slaves from Louisiana. He had been a student at a Bible School at Houston in Texas where a Methodist minister called Charles Parham had begun to teach 'baptism in the Spirit' with the expectation of speaking in tongues as an accompanying sign. Parham's own character was flawed by racial prejudice and at the Bible School Seymour was allowed to follow the lessons only through the half-open door of the classroom while he sat outside in the corridor.

When Seymour moved to Los Angeles he first held meetings in his home. But as people began to experience 'baptism in the Spirit' others crowded into the house so enthusiastically that it caved in. A new meeting place was found at 312 Azusa Street and this house became open day and night for worship, preaching and prayer and was the scene of a revival which lasted three years.

Seymour was a gentle man. He did not use the oratory characteristic of the black preaching tradition. He spoke like a teacher giving instruction and then invited the Spirit to come and do what he wanted. So great was his desire for self-effacement that he sometimes just hid his head in one of the wooden shoeboxes of which the pulpit was made. Both white and black people met at his meetings, something quite exceptional in Los Angeles at the beginning of the century, certainly under a black leader. He himself believed that the reconciliation of the races was a special feature of what God was bringing about.

Thousands came to visit, some from Canada, Great Britain and other parts of the world. The Pentecostal movement spread dramatically through the States and beyond, sometimes through the direct influence of those who had been to Azusa Street and sometimes through apparently spontaneous events elsewhere. Visitors included theologians such as Thomas Barratt and a scholarly Indian missionary called Pandita Rambai. Seymour's newspaper 'The Apostolic Faith' went round the world in an edition of 50,000 copies. The first issue carried the statement, 'We are not fighting against people or churches but we are seeking to replace dead forms and dogmas with a living practical Christianity'.

Pentecostal and charismatic movements have been a powerful expression of Christian vitality. They have exemplified attitudes which marked many earlier renewal movements, in heartfelt appeal to God for the demonstration of his presence and activity. They have been the means by which millions of men and women of varied race and culture have been drawn into personal assurance of God's love in Jesus, transformation of character, committed Christian discipleship and its practical outworking, capacity to speak, do and suffer for the Gospel's sake.

There has been plenty of variety. As with many renewal movements there have been pathways from fresh beginnings towards greater institutionalisation. There have been varied stances on all sorts of questions of theology and Christian living, including spiritual gifts. (Many people in Pentecostal churches and in the charismatic movement have not allowed praying in tongues the level of importance that was often given to it in the excitement of the initial revival). Pentecostalism has shown a great capacity for the acceptance of culture. People could become Christians without having to abandon their own identity and traditions and yet their identity and traditions have also been profoundly impacted by the Gospel.

Numerical growth is not the proper measure of a cause's inherent truth. Many non-Pentecostal churches have grown vigorously as well. But the statistics of Pentecostalism are still remarkable. The movements it embraced grew to a size numbering perhaps 400 million people worldwide by the start of the 21st century.[8] It is anticipated that before long the number of Pentecostals will exceed that of the total membership of the Protestant churches. Two-thirds of these are in the Third World and often in unexpected places.

Throughout the twentieth century many people in mainstream churches had some degree of dislike and suspicion of Pentecostal and charismatic movements, associating them with high emotionalism or an excessive attachment to the irrational. There has often been some justification for dislike. Positive appreciation here is not intended as generalised approval of everything which different people within these streams have done or said. Authentic experience of God and his Spirit may often be accompanied by immaturity and mistakes. Vigorous revivals are attended by hazards and the attitudes shown by leaders are of critical importance.

The New Testament, which itself arose out of the dynamic growth experiences of the early church, constantly offers its own relevant guidelines. In his letters to the church in Corinth Paul addresses a community whose chaotic worship, heady triumphalism and divisive rivalries did require his careful correction. Even this was a church which he sincerely appreciated for all its evidence of lives transformed by knowledge of Jesus and full of genuine gifts and enrichment (1 Cor. 1.3-9).

My wife and I were part of a group which went to Nepal in 2001 visiting the leaders of a group of indigenous churches in the Gorkha region. We met Christians of remarkable faith, courage and experience. These churches had grown out of the ministry of one man who became a Christian in the 1970s, after his wife had been dramatically healed of life-threatening illness through prayer offered in the name of Jesus. He had subsequently travelled tirelessly round rural villages to preach, to pray for the sick and to begin building small communities of committed disciples.

Jose Comblin is a Belgian Catholic who has lived and worked in Latin America since 1958. He is the author of over 40 books, including one published in 1989 called 'The Holy Spirit and Liberation'. This focuses especially on the emergence of grassroots Christian communities where there is 'living experience of the Spirit in thousands upon thousands of small groups'.

The experiences to which I am referring are experiences of an unexpected transformation. People feel themselves taken over by new strength that makes them do things they had never thought of doing. Individuals and communities that had been downhearted, lacking in dynamism, resigned to the endless struggle for survival, discover themselves to be protagonists of a history far greater than themselves. [9]

The ministry of John Wimber

I have referred to the origins of modern Pentecostalism in southern California, although it spread rapidly to other parts of the world and took root in localised settings. Southern California was also the home of a man of the later twentieth century who had a remarkable worldwide influence. John Wimber was a Californian pastor whose own local fellowship adopted the name of 'Vineyard' in 1982. Other fellowships under the same name became established elsewhere in the States and in due course in other parts of the world. But he cared deeply for the Church of Christ in every part and his worldwide travels profoundly affected churches of many denominations.

Of course American Christianity is hugely varied. English Christians sometimes associate it with styles of which they are suspicious, especially of religious showmanship or a nationalistic brand of politics. These are not the relevant images for the life and ministry of John Wimber. He did often appear a controversial figure, an object of criticism, suspicion and sometimes extreme misrepresentation. He bore these with great patience. Others deeply admired him but he always discouraged any tendency to heroise him and exposed his own normality, struggles and mistakes. He was full of humour.

His teaching and example were rich in basic New Testament themes – personal assurance of God's saving love through the work of Christ on the cross, the pursuit of Christlikeness of character, the centrality of worship and prayer, the Holy Spirit's equipping ordinary Christians for varied ministries, the necessity of loving and supportive relationships within the Body of Christ and active concern for the poor and downtrodden. He was a natural leader with great gifts in encouraging the development of young leaders. He had an instinctive wisdom in issues to do with church growth and a desire for the church to relate to people in culture-current ways. He learned to combine these with a prayerful reliance on God working by his Spirit.

He was a convert out of what he called the 'pagan pool', with no family background in Christianity.[10] He had been a musician with a band called the Righteous Brothers. His initially slow and stumbling absorption of Christian truths owed much to the patience and integrity of a house group leader. From being a convert John Wimber himself became a natural evangelist who drew many other people of his acquaintance into faith and commitment. From being an evangelist and pastor he became a consultant in church growth at Fuller Theological Seminary. He visited dozens of denominations across the States and advised several thousand pastors.

During these years he had colleagues who were studying the trends of world mission and he personally met many Third World Christian leaders who testified to supernatural 'signs and wonders' of all kinds alongside dramatic church growth. Previously he had had reservations about charismatic gifts but now he thought afresh about things that had already occurred in his own evangelistic work. Sometimes there had been unexplained insights into people's lives, perhaps into deep-seated hurt or other relevant circumstance, and by this means they became receptive to hearing the Gospel.

In due course the effect of overwork and various currents of personal despair led to a particular time when on an aeroplane flight to Detroit he was inwardly crying out to God for help. That night in a hotel room he opened a Bible and found himself reading Psalm 61. 'From the end of the earth I call to you with a fainting heart. Lead me to the rock that is higher than I.' In the middle of the night he felt that God was speaking to him directly. 'John, I've seen your ministry and now I'm going to show you mine'.

He left his work at Fuller and returned home in 1978 to be the pastor of a small fellowship in which his wife and other family members were already involved. They had already developed something of their own style of worship, spending considerable periods in a flow of songs of a contemporary kind, often written by themselves and focusing especially on quiet intimacy with the Lord. John led the church on the only lines he knew, with an emphasis on teaching and fellowship. But he was also trying to let God be in charge, even though he did not find this easy. In particular he felt God was prompting him to pray for sick people and to persevere with this even when seeing no good result. Afterwards he believed that these months had been used to bring him to a still deeper and more self-emptied place of dependence on God's mercy.

Eventually it was as though some reservoir of power had finally been tapped as positive results began to flow in visible healing and in other ways. Worship and teaching were accompanied by simple prayers in the form 'Come Holy Spirit', inviting God to do what he wanted in touching and blessing and guiding people. The church had over 1000 members by 1981, when David Watson from England happened to visit them for the first time and became John's personal friend. By 1983 the church had over 4000 and was sprouting a number of new congregations elsewhere.

In early visits to England the ministry of John and his team deeply affected some Anglican churches, including St Andrews Chorleywood and Holy Trinity Brompton, which have each developed in their own way since. Both have had remarkable outreach effects, HTB through the Alpha course and St Andrews through the New Wine Conferences and the youth network called Soul Survivor.

John Wimber's book 'Power Evangelism' stressed the significance for Christian mission of expecting signs of God's presence and power regularly to accompany the preaching of the Gospel and the life of the Church. His subsequent book 'Power Healing' gave a full account of his belief, experience and procedures in the realm of prayer for the sick. In many quarters these 'power' emphases were heavily criticised and he revised the first book to clarify his views in face of misunderstanding.[11]

The 'power' label could indeed be misleading. It could suggest an aggressive edge to outreach, though Vineyard churches have been exemplary in welcoming people in a relaxed and friendly environment. It could suggest an obsession with the dramatic. In fact the 'signs' by which individuals are impressed may be events of a quite simple kind yet personally meaningful in communicating the reality of a loving and seeking God. 'Power' could suggest a distortion of the New Testament's emphasis on the theology of the Cross. But John Wimber knew plenty about the theology of the Cross, both in the preaching of the Gospel and in the importance of Christian acceptance of suffering. Out of his pastoral wisdom he offered consolation in suffering and the hope of heaven in face of death, as reflected in the booklet 'Living with uncertainty'.[12] This was written out of his own experience of cancer in 1992 and endurance of radiation treatment. He continued to battle with his own ill health until his death in 1997 at the age of 63.

He was an outstanding Christian practitioner. The strength of his leadership was seen in the quality of mind and life of many others whose ministry he stimulated and forwarded. A characteristic statement of Vineyard principles is: 'We do nothing for religious effect but we operate in natural low-key patterns, desiring to do the ministry of Christ with joy. We want to walk in the Spirit and see real supernatural works of God. We also aim to function on the natural plane based on God's leading in conjunction with good rational thinking'.

A visit to Anaheim

In 1990, not long after we had moved to Ivybridge in Devon, my wife Heather felt prompted to get up early on several successive mornings to spend time praying in church. She felt it had a relevance for the church's future. No particular sense of guidance came to her until, leaving the church one morning, she picked up a leaflet which she saw in the church vestibule. It was about a forthcoming Conference in Brighton arranged by John Wimber on the theme of 'Worship'. It was strange that we never got to know anyone in the church who was likely to have produced this leaflet and left it for the interest of others. Heather's attendance at this Conference was the beginning of our familiarity with John Wimber's ministry and with many people whom it had already influenced.

Near the end of 1994, as part of a longer stay in Southern California linked especially with the Vineyard Church in Lancaster on the edge of the desert, we spent two weeks in Anaheim in the Los Angeles urban area. Here we saw him in his role as Senior Pastor in his local church.

We enjoyed the varied texture of the Church's life, including Sunday worship with several thousand others and weekday attendance at many events including the small-scale fellowship of house groups. A striking bronze sculpture stands in the entrance hall, showing Jesus on his knees washing Peter's feet. A lot of love was evident within the church and outwards to others, including impoverished Spanish-speaking families in the immediate neighbourhood. We appreciated how much of the weekly programme was of loving ministry to adults in recovery, with specialised support groups for those recovering from drug-abuse or eating disorders or sexual addictions or trauma and with high standards of counselling skill.

This happened to be the time when phenomena at the Airport Vineyard Church at Toronto were attracting a lot of visitors and worldwide attention. Similar things happened at Anaheim also and there were currently evenings at the church where relaxed space was set aside for worship and prayer. Here those who wished could have great freedom in waiting on God and experiencing his presence, with a high degree of acceptance when some laughed or cried or shook or lay prostrate on the ground. Such things have been attested from many times and places in Church history but in 1994 they resulted in the Vineyard movement facing a lot of media publicity and worldwide controversy.

We were present at a meeting to which John Wimber had invited church leaders of other denominations in the local area and he spoke to them very humbly. He fully believed that there was a sovereign activity of God involved in the current events. He himself had been willing to allow things to occur without too rigorous restriction in order to have time to discern what was really significant. He had seen striking impact on people whom he knew well and whose integrity he knew. He believed that the fruit of what was happening was by and large overwhelmingly beneficial, visible in deeper devotion to Jesus, commitment to evangelism and capacity for compassionate service.

I can now add that for more than ten years the loving ministry of that community in Toronto has been offered continuously to the hundreds of thousands who have visited from all over the world. Anyone who wants to consider the whole phenomenon seriously can read the accounts published under the title 'Experience the Blessing'.[13] Here are the stories of more than twenty Christian leaders from many nations about the circumstances that took them there and how they encountered God in that place. Heidi Baker tells how exhausted she felt after sixteen years of missionary work and how she spent hours lying on the floor in Toronto, experiencing the weight of God's presence and the depth of Jesus' love. She describes the extraordinary subsequent development of the work she shares with her husband in Mozambique, the care for hundreds of orphan children, the commitment to feeding thousands during massive flooding, the spiritual hunger of the people as well as their physical hunger, a six week period when twelve thousand became Christians, the planting of several hundred new churches.

I have not been to Toronto but Heather went for four days. She spoke in our church on the following Sunday evening. The church was decorated for Harvest Festival. She was so happy about the beauty of things she had heard and seen. I felt very happy too. That night just before sleeping I opened my Bible with a sense of gratitude to God. The words to which my eyes directly came were from Psalm 4, 'You have put more joy in my heart than they had when their corn and wine increased'.

All through Christian history there are places which have become special for many because of the experience of God's presence there. God has used these places. Of course we know perfectly well that God also saves us from excessive attachment to places and that we must seek his presence everywhere.

In 1994, close to the end of our two weeks in the Vineyard Church in Anaheim, I sat quietly for a while in the large worship area, filled with people on a Sunday but now quite empty in the middle of a weekday morning. Spontaneously I prayed and said 'Lord, thank you for your presence here'. Then for a split second I was strongly aware of God's extraordinary height and holiness. I was conscious of him at an immense distance, above the church, above Los Angeles, above the world, beyond the solar system, beyond the universe. In the same instant I knew that from where he was there was a corridor of immediate access, a beam of instant presence, down to that particular church but also down to everywhere where he is able to make himself known.

I do not mean that God's true home is in a physical location, however distant. Distance is still only a metaphor for the difference between his dimension and ours. But the rapid picture expressed to me afresh the mystery of the one to whom Jesus taught us to pray. 'Our Father in heaven, your name be hallowed, your Kingdom come'. He is the one whose purposes keep on running forward. He urges us to seek him. 'Lord, do what you want, do what you please, do what you purpose. Your will be done on earth, as it is in heaven'.

7. 'LORD, TEACH US TO PRAY'

The effects of prayer

A CHINESE teenager longed to possess a copy of the Bible and read the words of Jesus for himself. This was in the aftermath of the Cultural Revolution of the 1960s and Bibles simply could not be found. He began to pray on a daily basis, 'Lord, give me a Bible'. For four months he persisted in this prayer, sometimes surviving on a minimum of food to intensify his prayer by fasting. Eventually one morning he answered a knock at the door and two strangers handed him a bag. An evangelist in a village at a great distance had seen a vision of a young man to whom he was to give a Bible and in his vision had seen the location of the village and the particular house. He had delayed for three months before deciding to be obedient to the instruction but had finally arranged for two others to make the delivery.

This incident is taken from 'The Heavenly Man', a book which many Western Christians have read since its publication in 2002.[1] It is the story of Liu Zhenying, more commonly known as Brother Yun, who grew up in poverty in the Chinese province of Henan and became an outstanding evangelist with a major role in the growth of the house church movement in China. He suffered three periods of imprisonment and prolonged torture prior to a remarkable escape in 1997. Since that time he has been mainly in the West, although in 2001 he endured a further imprisonment in Myanmar where he had travelled in hope of rejoining his wife and family who were in hiding there. A constant theme of his ministry is his vision for the mobilisation of large numbers of Chinese missionaries equipped to work in other countries.

The tone of the book is recognisably that of the New Testament, both in the account of 'signs and wonders' and in the willingness for suffering as a consequence of obedience to the gospel. The central focus is neither on miracles nor on suffering but on devotion to the God revealed in Jesus. Sometimes God is known as mysteriously present even in extremities of pain. Sometimes he brings help and rescue even against all expectation. Through everything he calls for faith that he is ultimately worthy of love and trust. Yun's book is a testimony to the power of prayerfulness, both in the building of intimacy with God and in the evidence of requests made and answered.

It is easy to understand the scepticism which affects people of Christian commitment as well as those who abandon any sort of faith commitment. Claims of answered prayer can seem hollow beside the observed realities of ongoing human suffering. There is always a pressure, both for philosophical theologians and for others, to suppose that after all we cannot look for God to intervene in the course of events. A church where I started serving as minister had kept a Prayer Request book in which anyone might write subjects for intercession. But use of the book had been abandoned for at least a year. In the final entry someone had requested prayer for a man who was ill but in the margin someone else had added the stark update 'He died'.

Countless reliably recorded instances show that prayers do get answered. It would be possible to maintain that strange events occur for people of all faiths and none (because of telepathic or other forces not easy to quantify scientifically) but that they are not a secure guide to what is ultimately true. So we cannot compel the belief of others. We know that there are mysteries in the nature of God's presence and activity in a suffering world and large questions in the relationship of Christian belief with the varied and shifting levels of scientific understanding. Yet the Bible provides us with practical guidance for living in the world in a prayerful way, learning to pray with maturity but also with expectation.

Some Christians annoy other people when they describe intimate ways they think God has blessed them. 'I had tried to become a Christian at school, but been put off by someone coming in to talk to the Christian Union and explaining that God had sent them a pastel green Volvo estate car'. So writes the actress Sally Phillips as a prelude to describing her later conversion.[2] Some Christians can be too zealous in looking for special providences and liable to be mistaken. But these are not serious arguments for simply discounting remarkable answers to prayer.

The Chinese Christian to whom I've referred comments on his own dramatic career by saying:

In China the greatest miracles we see are not the healings or other things but lives transformed by the gospel. We believe we're not called to follow signs and wonders but instead the signs and wonders follow us when the

78

Gospel is preached. We don't keep our eyes on the signs and wonders, we keep our eyes on Jesus. Every house church pastor in China is ready to lay down his life for the gospel. When we live this way, we'll see God do great things by his grace.[3]

Many followers of other religions engage in prayer with a discipline and reverence which can be salutary for Christians to observe. Christian prayer is distinctive because it is addressed to God as Father according to the teaching of Jesus and it is based on intimate relationship with God experienced through the work of Jesus. Christian prayer is personal communication within this relationship. Prayer has many aspects, including the worship of God for who he is and thankfulness for his gifts. We know that it is not all a matter of requesting things. Prayer will constantly adjust our own attitudes and shape our actions. But this does not mean that its sole effect is the therapeutic massaging of our own minds.

Prayer and healing

I conducted the wedding of a young couple called John and Sonia on Easter Saturday 1972, during my first year in active ministry. They were not churchgoers and their only link with the life of the chapel where they were married was that John's grandmother was a loyal member. By way of preparation we had talked about the meaning and the practicalities of the marriage commitment. I had also told them my own conviction about Christianity as personal relationship with God.

John was taken ill the day after the wedding with symptoms that were first thought to point to epilepsy. Before long a brain tumour was diagnosed and he started a period of many months in and out of hospital. I went to visit him on several occasions. I don't think I ever suggested to him that I would pray with him for healing. In private I was regularly praying that he might be healed. He did spontaneously start asking me a lot of questions about God, not embittered ones about his predicament but the searching questions of someone seriously in pursuit of faith. I gave what answers I could but had no idea in what particular way he might come through this seeking phase into a sense of discovery.

One day I visited him in hospital and he wanted to tell me what had happened the previous day. Apparently he had been drowsy, in and out of sleep, and a man he didn't know had come and stood by his bed and said 'It is time to give your heart to the Lord'. I did not gather how long the man stayed or what else he might have said. The impression I got was simply 'A man came and said this and so I did it'. I was bewildered about who this strange pastoral visitor could have been. I certainly never met him and John never mentioned him again.

John died a few weeks later. From the intervening time I remember the quiet unassuming clarity I saw in him of having moved into a place of knowing God for himself. Without doubt this was a transforming factor for him in coping with his sorrow and the sorrow of his wife and family.

My sense of surprise at how God had worked went hand in hand with accepting that my prayers for his healing were not answered. Not long afterwards, with this and other instances on my mind, I talked to an elderly minister who had a considerable experience of healing ministry. He told me that the whole area remained mysterious to him. He had sometimes seen extraordinary things happen before his eyes as he laid hands on people and prayed for them. But there were no guarantees of any kind. Currently his own wife was very ill. Various Christian friends had come to him saying they had prayed for her and were sure she was going to be healed. But he had no personal conviction about it.

Now more than thirty years later my wife and I readily remember some remarkable instances of physical healing. One involved a young mother who had already had several years of debilitating long-term illness. We kept company with her over many months as we saw God working in her life and leading her into a place of worshipping him more profoundly regardless of her own well-being. But one day while having my morning cup of coffee I was suddenly sure we should gather together a group of people from the church and pray with her for her healing. We arranged this with her full consent and straight afterwards she was well again and resumed a new level of life and career activity.

When such things have happened we have rejoiced in them. Of course we do not dream of generalising that everyone is going to be healed of their infirmities if only 'believing' prayers are offered. Even experiences of 'sudden sureness' should only be taken as promptings to pray, not as promises of healing made to others. Marked improvements in anyone's health should be viewed as subject to medical confirmation and the test of time.

It is right for Christians to live exactly within the terms which Paul's Epistles prescribe out of the experience of the very first Christian generation. Luke is the 'beloved doctor' and medical resource and dedication are gifts from God. There are also times when healing is experienced beyond medical resource, as it was so often in the ministry of Jesus, and some Christians have particular aptitude in this ministry even though the source of healing is God himself and not human giftedness. Paul saw remarkable things happen at his own hands (as he testifies in 1 Corinthians 12.12 and as Luke's account in the Acts of the Apostles endorses). But Paul also clearly views the Christian life as lived out within experiences of weakness of which the frustration of physical infirmity is one category. Famously he records an intimate experience of God telling him 'My grace is sufficient for you'. This was in a severe personal affliction (we are not told its exact nature) where he had solemnly prayed three times for release (2 Corinthians 12.7-9).

My wife and I prayed with a lady who was troubled with a rash, a nasty and persistent one which had repeatedly defied diagnosis or treatment. We didn't know and couldn't promise that God would take it away in answer to prayer. But we suggested that we should at least ask God's help and guidance. She was partly willing and partly hesitant, typical of many Christians who regard their own discomforts as minor and hardly right to trouble God about. But with Paul's example in mind we suggested we would pray with her briefly on three occasions.

After the third time she told us that she'd had a dream. In the dream she saw a little matchstick figure of a person and a large hand above with a finger reaching down. The little person was jumping up and down to try to touch the big finger, at first very feebly but gradually jumping with more and more resolve until finally a contact was made. She believed it carried a message about reaching out to God whose love and power are there for us. Then over a period of weeks the rash disappeared, absolutely steadily but so gradually that the recovery would never have made it into the Guinness Book of Amazing Miracles. Even where God works the door is regularly left open for either faith or unbelief.

Is it 'unfair' that God apparently allows one person to be healed and not another, seems to rescue one and not another? Yes, it can seem as unfair as life itself can seem unfair. (In terms of the eleventh chapter of Hebrews I would rather be rescued from the mouth of a lion than sawn in two). But as committed Christians we have all signed away our right to life anyway. 'Whether we live or die, we belong to the Lord' (Romans 14.8). This is more than pious resignation. It is a reality of relationship with God. Whether we are healthy or afflicted, successful or struggling, we belong to him and need intimacy with him.

For me the quite primitive picture of the matchstick figure jumping to reach the big finger applies beyond the realm of healing into other areas where we need to call out to God.

Prayer and the renewal of the Church

From the New Testament we remember the period of days between the final appearance of the Risen Jesus to his gathered disciples and the dramatic events which affected them at the pilgrim-feast of Pentecost. Luke tells us that during these days a total company of 120 men and women stayed together in prayerful anticipation.

In Church history there is a constant link between prayer and renewal. A significant event in the origins of Methodism was a meeting in Fetter Lane in London on the evening of January 1st 1739.[4] The record of this meeting shows the dedicated prayerfulness with which about sixty people, including George Whitefield and the Wesley brothers, together worshipped God and pleaded for his activity in the life of the nation. The meeting continued all night and at three o'clock in the morning those present were overwhelmed by an exceptional sense of God's presence, power and majesty. Prayer was the environment in which, over succeeding months and years, a dynamic activity of God became visible in drawing others into Christian conviction and into the corporate life of the Church. Prayer was an enterprise in which people were conscious of co-operating with God for ends which could simply not have been achieved by their unaided activity or well-meaning.

The whole impact of the Moravian Christians on the Wesley brothers links back to the Moravian experience in prayer. A German aristocrat Count Zinzendorf had allowed Christians who were refugees from various parts of Europe to settle on his estate at Herrenhut in Germany. At first this diverse community was full of animosities and fractiousness. A new spirit of reconciliation came in the summer of 1727, when gathered at a Communion service they

82

were powerfully affected by the expression of God's love in the Cross of Christ. At the end of August twenty-four men and twenty-four women of the community covenanted together to spend one hour each day, day and night, in prayer to God for His blessing on the congregation and its witness. This practice of non-stop intercession by hourly rota continued for a hundred years. Already within fifteen years the Moravians had established missions in the Virgin Islands, Greenland, Turkey, the Gold Coast of Africa, South Africa and North America.

The Moravian hundred-year 'prayer meeting' is of renewed significance today in the direct inspiration which it has given to the Christian youth movement called 24-7. Pete Greig, a worker in a Southampton church, visited Herrenhut in 1999. Inspired by the visit he asked young people at his church to pray continuously for a month. He says it seemed like a good idea until he realized how many hours there are in a month. The church leaders and most of the young people were afraid it would be simply exhausting, but they eventually agreed to give it a try and established a prayer room. The young people learned about Zinzendorf and the Moravian revival. The one-month event lasted three months. 'The thing went absolutely crazy,' Pete says. 'People who had hardly prayed in their lives were staying up all night. People came to the room just to sit because they could sense the presence of God.' Artistic gifts began to come forth as people turned their prayers into poems and songs and the room filled up with paintings, graffiti, heart-rending prayers and prophecy. [5]

Spontaneously and informally the movement has grown, influencing many other churches and groups nationwide and worldwide. Groups pick a period of maybe a week or a month and arrange for people to pray in a designated room in shifts around the clock. People ask God to bless their families, friends and peers, to bless the life and outreach of the churches and to work by his Spirit in local and national situations. Groups are invited to register with the 24/7 web site which features accounts of past events, inspirational stories and prayer needs from around the world.

A participant in Northampton wrote: 'Our prayer room in Northampton is mad, crazy, outrageous, contagious, deep, real - we can hardly describe it. God is really here. We walked into the room and could feel God's presence, almost as if something was brushing against your skin.'

24-7 prayer rooms are not just in churches. They may be in skate parks, deserted buildings, farmhouses or nightclubs. Pete Greig has written:

The goal is to turn the tide among youth. Many young people are living on the edge, seeking thrills in a frenzy of partying and risky entertainment, and most are turning away from church. The body of Christ in the West is bleeding young people....

Young people get involved in the prayer movement because they see the spiritual impact. This takes prayer out of the hands of intercessory specialists and puts it in the hands of normal people. Interacting with Christians in other countries through 24-7's website gives them the feeling that they are part of a family and are taking part in a global move of God. There is a sense that God is doing this and we are running to catch up.

God is doing things and we must run to catch up. He does not call only to those of particular age or inclination. The Methodist Church in Britain, because of a request from young people influenced by the 24-7 prayer movement, designated the year from June 2005 to August 2006 as a special period of prayer under the title 'Pray without ceasing'. At the time of writing, with much of the period still to run, I hope that many in Methodist churches will respond to this call as a matter of the highest significance.

The Methodist Church in Cuba has grown dramatically in recent years, its membership increasing from a low point of less than a thousand to at least 20,000 with hundreds of new church plants. The majority of members and pastors are under the age of 30. The Bishop, Ricardo Pereira Diaz, has witnessed at first hand the connection between dedicated prayerfulness and the sovereign activity of God. [6]

In the 1960s it was very hard for us. Only 5 pastors out of 140 remained. Our membership went down. The 70s also were very hard years. In the 1980s our church started to awake. We found our refuge in God. Our church began prayer and fasting. From the late 1980s we have been experiencing the power and presence of the Holy Spirit in the name of Jesus Christ.

Managing to pray as we can

When giving time to pray, whether shorter or longer, a simple pattern which I often use is based on four elements - worship, Word, wanting and waiting.

- Worship - speaking to the God revealed in Jesus and affirming his presence, his truth and his love. (Perhaps use recorded worship music that helps to focus you).

- Word - according to a reading plan or in a more spontaneous way, consider a verse or verses from the Bible, asking God to help you with their meaning, perhaps turning the words into a prayer that you can pray back to him.

- Wanting - this word is chosen for the sake of the alliteration but it covers the 'requests' that Paul tells us to make known to God (Phil. 4). Make requests for yourself and for those whose needs are on your heart and for the life and mission of the Church. Use pen and paper if it helps. Above all pray 'Lord, do as you want, do as you purpose'.

- Waiting - ask that your mind may be open to God for what he wants to communicate to you, now or in a time of his choosing, in whatever way he wants to bring it. (More on listening to God in the next chapter).

Even those of us who have learned to treat prayer as important know that we do not find it wholly easy. We are familiar with the difficulties of giving it time, the difficulties of concentration even where time has been allowed. But we press on, because nothing else substitutes for the possibility and privilege of speaking personally with God. We recognise our shortcomings in the business of prayer but repeat the plea of Jesus' original disciples, 'Lord, teach us to pray'.

A collection of talks given by a variety of speakers at Holy Trinity Brompton includes a reflection on prayer from a member of that church called Glenda Waddell.[7] She had sat through a service in which people were challenged to give serious space to intercession.

I had felt more and more uncomfortable and thought I heard God saying, 'I've given you so much. Won't you do this thing for me?' All the time, another voice was saying. 'You couldn't do that. It would be doomed to failure from the beginning. You're not the intercessory type. Let someone else do it who's got more time'. At that time I think I was probably busier than I'd ever been and I was really tired. I couldn't believe that God would ask me to do this.

In the end she said, 'Lord, if you really want me to do this, will you wake me?' To her horror next morning she found herself sitting bolt upright at 5 am. She went downstairs and sat in a chair with a cup of coffee and said, 'Lord, I don't honestly know what to do. I don't know what intercession is. I don't know how to do intercession but if you want me to do it, I'll do it'. She started to pray and she didn't find it easy but she did have impressions that God was encouraging her. 'I need people who are just prepared to pray. I'll do the rest'.

She had often thought, 'God's got it all in control anyway. What's the point in going on and on about it to him? He knows it. He's got the answers. He must get pretty bored with us asking'. She had to pray that God would remove her apathy. Slowly she began to have a heart for things which God put in her mind. She began to see things supernaturally in a way that she hadn't before. In her personal life and in praying with others she felt more evidence of God's power. 'It was nothing that I did. It all came out of the intercession'.

Having spoken of John Wimber as someone who has affected so many by the quality of his character and ministry, I quote also from comments which he made about his own prayer life.[8] His total conviction about the place of prayer in Christian life was combined as ever with practical honesty and can encourage others who know they are not mighty prayer warriors. His own experience as a new Christian of setting the alarm early in the morning to start the day with prayer was that over two weeks he discovered that he could fall asleep in any position - standing, kneeling, sitting or in process of switching off the alarm. He got so discouraged.

I've not yet come to that place where I can pray for two or three hours at a time. Fifteen or twenty minutes is maximum for me at a time. Two or three minutes is normal at a time. But I can pray two to three minutes many times throughout the day. I find as I sleep at night, that I pray. I wake up praying sometimes... I pray often as I talk to people I meet throughout the course of my day. Talking to God has become as natural as breathing to me. It's as much a part of my thought life as any other aspect of my life.

No one becomes an expert at prayer overnight. We all experience false starts and seasons of dryness. You just have to pick yourself up and start all over again. If I had to pray hours and hours on end to go to heaven I couldn't go. I thank God it's not a requirement.

But he stresses the plain positive also. 'God has a desire for us to draw close to him. When you petition him it's his pleasure, his joy to answer your prayers. He enjoys the dialogue you have with him. He himself is the reward for that kind of prayer.'

I know that we cannot prescribe for each other the exact pathways of our own vocation. Some can follow their determination to dedicate fresh periods of time to sustained prayer, on their own or with others. Some can deepen their prayerfulness within the encounters and circumstances of everyday life and the quiet stretches of night-time wakefulness.

Through the period of writing these chapters I continue to feel the power of God's overall prescription for us.

God is working in fulfilment of his purpose, devising things that shall be, appealing in every possible way:
> **Turn to me.**
> **Call to me.**
> **Hope in me.**

8. LISTENING TO GOD

Scripture and inspiration

WHEN our son was doing 'A' Levels he lost a piece of course work which needed to be handed in next day. We searched all over the house with no result. In the end we prayed as a family that God would show us where it was. The only thing Stephen thought he could hear God saying was 'Worship me'. So he went off to his bedroom to find his guitar and a file of music. Here between sheets of music he found his coursework.

Such an instance could be interpreted as a flash of clairvoyance or subconscious memory without clear relevance to issues of theology. But this seems strange considering that it came as an answer to a heartfelt prayer offered in the name of Jesus and involving a call to worship. I know such an instance can seem trivial in the light of the world's larger calamities. Should we expect God to intervene on our behalf whenever we lose something? Should we expect him to give instant answers to every perplexity? Clearly not. Christian intimacy with God through Jesus is not dependent on constant special guidance or easy resolution of difficulties. But neither should we despise the times when practical help comes in surprising ways in answer to prayer. Sometimes God reveals his presence by particular evidences and at other times he calls us to trust his presence even in the hardest places on the basis of biblical promises. Our son understands both sides of this. He is now in his late twenties and since 2001 has been a missionary in the north of Burkina Faso in sub-Saharan Africa.[1]

Many Christians have had experiences, in large or small instances, where they believe God has guided them by impressions. Sometimes it is a Bible verse or passage which comes into the mind with specific force. Anything which comes authentically from God must certainly correspond with his character and activity as known from the New Testament.

Christians are agreed that the Bible is a widely varied collection of documents written by human beings in historical settings. The Old Testament is the Jewish scripture compiled over a period of centuries and the New Testament is a Christian supplement of various writings from the first century AD. Through both Old and New Testament there are numerous questions as to what is of universal and timeless relevance for Christians and what has to be understood as limited to an original context of particular culture. It is clear that elements of the Old Testament record are radically re-evaluated by Jesus himself, such as the sometimes vindictive treatment of enemies or any tendency to see material prosperity as an anticipated reward for righteous living. Debates about biblical interpretation will always be with us. But it remains the Church's primary resource for the knowledge of God and his revelation in Jesus.

I have never been impressed by any claim for the Bible's literal 'infallibility' but neither have I ever been persuaded by attitudes of extreme scepticism. The letters of Paul are written within the first generation after Easter and the Gospels derive directly from the eyewitness memories recounted within this same generation. Some scholars with a basic aversion to crediting anything miraculous have been far too ready to believe that episodes of the New Testament story were simply invented. Even when I had much more limited perception of God's miraculous working throughout Christian history I basically believed in the New Testament miracles. To put it crudely, if Jesus did not do things which created astonishment then it is difficult to understand why he was regarded as such an extraordinary person that extraordinary stories were created about him.

I have done a lot of academic study of the Bible. But I have already shown that the Bible itself, discussed with others and read in private, was a primary means by which I became freshly awakened to God's living reality. It is only within this context of reverence for Scripture that I make frequent mention in these pages of other experiences of hearing from God.

A few years ago a young Christian talked to me about his terrible sense of shame over something which he had done. Theoretical knowledge of God's willingness to forgive seemed powerless to release him from the darkness of the place into which he had fallen. After a short time of conversation I suggested we would be silent together for a couple of minutes and offer the situation to God without many words. In this silence just two words came into my consciousness and they were 'Deep Grace'. They surprised me by their clarity. The words just seemed to come from God's own heart and to affirm that whatever the depth of a problem his capacity to resolve it would reach deeper. Deeper than ordinary forgiveness there is extraordinary forgiveness. Deeper than the love we anticipate from God is the unanticipated level of his love. I shared this briefly and it seemed to register. It registered with me. I felt I had touched the actuality of what Paul describes in Romans 5.22, that 'where sin abounded, grace hyper-exceeded it'.

Many Christians with pastoral or evangelistic ministries have had their own evidences of divine prompting. Unfortunately there is no shortage of other instances where Christians even with the best of intentions have behaved or spoken foolishly on the basis of what they believed God was telling them. Impressions may come from anywhere in the murk of the subconscious. There is no question of conceding that everything that pops into the mind unexpectedly is from God. We have to attempt judgements on grounds of Scripture and reason and the significance of any recognisable psychological factors.

In my early years of ministry I experienced a situation where someone in a church was more than once standing up to address a Sunday morning congregation in the middle of worship time, in order to present messages which he sincerely believed were from God and felt commissioned to proclaim. I was so concerned not to quench anything genuine and so unused to how such things might best be handled that I did not give good leadership in this case. Even if there was significant content in what he had to say I should not have given him as much licence as I did. Leaders must take responsibility for how and when to allow others to speak and those who claim any sort of prophetic awareness should respect leadership. Jesus did call out in public without invitation on the final day of the Feast of Tabernacles, but that is not the norm for Christian fellowship.

The evidence of Scripture and history [2]

Paul did not know a form of Church life in which prophecy was not experienced. In 1 Corinthians he encourages all church members to 'seek to prophesy' (14.1), even though he knew how unwisely excitable this particular congregation could get about spiritual phenomena if left to their own devices.

Beyond the specific attitudes of Paul the experience of 'hearing from God' can be tracked right through the Scriptural record. Indeed it supplies a considerable amount of the content of the Scriptural record. From Abraham and Moses to Samuel and Elijah and the whole succession of prophets whose output is recorded from Isaiah to

Malachi, people gifted to hear what God is saying are entrusted with guiding and guarding the life of his people. In some places in the Old Testament there appears an expression of hope that hearing from God would be a very widespread experience not confined to special gifted individuals. In Numbers 11.29 Moses says 'I wish that all the Lord's people were prophets'. In Joel 2.28 the gift of prophecy is the first mentioned evidence of the future pouring out of the Spirit 'on all flesh'.

Jesus warns against false prophets and their destructive impact when they claim to speak from God but are misguided and manipulative (Matthew 7.15). But his warning against the counterfeit shows the value which he sets on the authentic. He passionately grieves over Israel's rejection of many true prophets (Luke 13.34).

In the New Testament record John the Baptist and Jesus himself are both acknowledged as prophets. The Gospel of John presents Jesus' words and actions as constantly guided by what he 'hears' from the Father. His constant closeness of communication with God is a reflection of the uniqueness of relationship with him which he enjoyed by his own divine origin. But he is also in his humanity, anointed by the Spirit of God, the model for our own humanity touched by the Spirit of God. We must listen to God through the recorded words and actions of Jesus but we can also learn something about listening in the way that Jesus himself listened.

Regularly in Church history there have been times and places where groups got carried away by excitement over their own 'illuminations'. In the second century Montanus and his female associates launched a movement strongly proclaiming prophetic gifting but bizarre in its messages. Apparently it was even claimed that Montanus was himself the 'Paraclete' who Jesus had promised and the end of the world was shortly to come in Asia Minor. A strongly ascetic teaching was offered contradicting the spirit of Jesus' own teaching.

Martin Luther in the sixteenth century, for all his Protestant emphasis on obedience to the inward witness of the Spirit, found himself in opposition to groups which were devaluing Scripture by their stress on daily revelations. Thomas Muntzer, a radical figure of the time, is reported to have countered Luther's reference to the Bible by saying 'What Bible? One must withdraw into a corner and speak with God'. John Calvin encountered 'spiritualists' claiming a form of

Christian perfection which allowed them to rely solely on the Holy Spirit for guidance. In practice the results were immorality and anarchy.

In reaction against extremism there has often been an endeavour to shut down on the idea of individuals hearing from God. Montanism led to official insistence on confining gifts of prophecy, preaching and teaching to properly prepared and ordained male clergy. The sixteenth-century Reformers pointed strongly to the exposition of Scripture through authorised preachers. With the best of motives they left a legacy which diminished the congregational interaction allowed in the New Testament churches.

In the eighteenth century Wesley's caution about being guided by impressions was increased because of the erratic claims of extreme enthusiasts. Wesley rightly asserted the importance of reason, Scripture and the fruit of the Spirit in Christian living. But he also gave strong encouragement to lay ministry, stressed the role of the Spirit in guiding the actions of believers and definitely reflected on the possibility of God restoring to the Church more of the 'extraordinary' gifts that appeared to be so familiar in the early Church.[3]

At many times and places in Christian history there is evidence of the authentic power of the prophetic. We find people who kept utmost reverence for the authority of Scripture being also specifically led by the kind of communications from God that Scripture itself so often records. These include great saintly names such as Augustine, Patrick, Bernard of Clairvaux, Francis of Assisi. They include pioneers of the Church of Scotland, within a strong Reformation pattern of preaching and teaching but displaying supernatural gifts in their mission and ministry. They include numerous Christians of no special distinction who have lived in personal closeness to God, often in the middle of tasks of mission and ministry and compassionate self-giving.

A familiar hymn by Frances Ridley Havergal, 'Master, speak, thy servant heareth', is a classic expression of openness to God's voice, without prescribing too closely in what way we will get to hear it. The power of the hymn is independent of the biographical details of its author. But she had regular awareness of hearing God speak and it was a common experience in her hymn-writing that she wrote by inspiration rather than by conscious effort.

Misconceptions in prophecy

David Parker is now pastor of the Vineyard Church in Lancaster in Southern California. He was converted to Christianity at the time of the 'Jesus People' movement in the late 1960s. He had been immersed in hippie culture. The conversion of a close friend to Christianity led him into reading the Bible for himself so that he could demonstrate its errors and persuade his friend that he had been brainwashed. After jumping straight into the book of the Leviticus, a bewildering beginning for his venture, he was advised by someone that he would do better to read the Gospel of John. This had a considerable impact on him, which he described as turning him from atheism to agnosticism. Later, reading backwards through parts of the Old Testament he came upon Isaiah 53 which profoundly persuaded him that he had been personally rejecting the one whom God had sent.

From such a starting-point he became a considerable biblical scholar but also a preacher and pastor deeply intent on natural and attractive ways of expressing Christian faith to people who are searching for life's meaning. He has had a remarkable ability to hear God's voice in prophetic ways and to encourage others to appreciate prophetic things.

My wife and I were among a group of ministers and spouses to whom he once spoke in London in 1992, at a time when he was living and working in England. After talking to us together he came to each of us individually and spent a few moments praying quietly with us and telling us whatever he believed God was saying. The accuracy of some of the supernatural knowledge which was displayed and the beauty of some of the encouragement given was breathtaking. Yet this was someone who on principle was extremely cautious about 'prophecy on demand', where Christians end up regularly looking around for a prophetic person who can give them a special word. Much of the time he would rather they pressed on with ordinary Christian motivations – read your Bible, honour your marriage, work hard, love your neighbour, give generously, think things through.

On another occasion a couple of years later we heard him give a talk called 'Mistakes in Prophecy', where a lot of positive content was organised under the heading of misconceptions that people can readily have.

- It is a misconception that God is not speaking in the same way that he used to. The Bible shows how many different ways he was able to speak to people other than reading the Bible. He is still speaking in these ways.

- It is a misconception that 'God speaks to other people but not to me'. Whatever the differences of kind and degree it is a great thing to hear from God for ourselves. We need a personal place of being led by the Spirit.

- It is a misconception that when God speaks it is always obviously God. People can want the Burning Bush, the fire in the sky, the golden telephone. Sometimes things are given with exceptional clarity. But at other times impressions come which can be less clear and need gentle evaluating but may still prove very significant.

- It is a misconception that if prophecy is from God it will be a hundred percent accurate. Listening to God is a learning process and mistakes can be made. Paul says 'Since you have eager desire, aspire to excel in gifts that build up the church' (1 Cor. 14.12). We can't excel without aspiring and we can't aspire without failing sometimes. But if we are careful any failure will be a minor discomfiture for ourselves rather than a major stumbling-block to others.

- It is a misconception that prophecy should always be spoken in the first person and preferably in unnatural language. We shouldn't try to import this out of the Old Testament. If we are shown something which is relevant to someone else it is better to say 'Does this mean anything to you?' than 'Thus says the Lord'.

- It is a misconception that if God speaks to me my first response is to speak it out, preferably publicly. Our first response should be in prayer back to God, whether there is anything to be done with it and if so when.

- It is a misconception that 'if God speaks to me that makes me a prophet'. People can easily get an inflated sense of their own importance. There is a difference between Christians who have some taste of these experiences and those who have a long and proven and trustworthy calling. (And these also need humility and a knowledge of their own fallibility).

This is the same kind of practical wisdom with which many others have spoken and written on this theme. The whole area must not ultimately be judged by our worst ever experience of what somebody said or did but by our best ever models of how the prophetic dimension can light up God's ways, his truth and his love.

Openness to the God who speaks

God speaks through the Bible. He has also given us reason and intellect and these gifts are to be used and sharpened. He can lead us by means of listening to others and by the accumulation of experience in life situations. When we do feel a prompting in something which comes to mind we may not always be able to determine too exactly whether it is a natural good thought, an unexplained intuition or a special touch of Holy Spirit revelation. But in this chapter I have given special attention to the prophetic because it is so closely related to the reason for my writing at all. As we give space to listening to God he speaks in ways that are vitally related to the renewal of the Church.

Openness to hearing God's voice is an aspect of openness to the Holy Spirit. In an earlier chapter I suggested as a helpful model the simplicity with which Catherine Marshall asked God for more of the Spirit in her own experience and expected to see an outcome of her prayer, while leaving it with him what form such an outcome might take.

During the period of writing this book I met for the first time a man who lives thirty miles away from us. He and his wife worship in a Methodist church. He has a secular job as a management training consultant and is completely rooted in the real world! At the end of a working day towards the end of 2004 he had a vision which lasted for three hours and totally surprised and enthralled him. Throughout this time he was in the company of Jesus, seeing Jesus and hearing

96

him. In one episode he saw himself in a clearing in a forest where Jesus invited him to spend considerable time just resting in his presence. There were many other episodes, dramatic demonstrations of practical truths about relating to Jesus constantly and about the whole army of people that Jesus is preparing, entirely focused on his leading. There was practical instruction for how to pray - be still, seek Jesus' presence, don't be quick with your own agenda, learn to listen to him.

Expecting God to speak to us is not a competition to achieve distinction in how dramatic the results might be. But God does reveal himself in ways of his choosing. What he gives to one is often further used to bring encouragement and help to others.

A book called 'Surprised by the Voice of God', written by a biblical scholar called Professor Jack Deere, includes his own story of how he entirely changed his mind about whether God speaks in unmediated ways today.[1] He comments that those who feel the whole area of the prophetic is too subjective may be exactly those who would benefit from this element in their Christian lives. They are the ones who have the least likelihood of being led into error because they are strongly intellectual in focus or strongly attached to the careful use of the Bible. Perhaps what they most need is a balancing influence of a more vital 'subjective' relationship with God in their daily lives.

We do not all need to become Quakers and make silent waiting on God the primary content of our worship. But sometimes in Christian fellowship we can spend periods of quietness together, covered by a simple prayer that the Holy Spirit would be present and bring anything he wants to people's minds. Out of this there may be things that can be briefly and appropriately shared. There does not need to be too strong an interrogation about the level of inspiration in any particular contribution. Interesting and creative and encouraging and sometimes awe-inspiring things can flow out of such times.

Recently, when leading an act of Sunday morning worship in a local church, I spoke on the theme of listening to God. Afterwards, during a period of quietness in prayer, my wife was aware of two distinct pictures coming to her mind. Both were to do with water. One was a picture of people in a rainstorm wearing waterproof clothing, clearly uncomfortable with the wetness and huddling up to protect themselves as far as possible. The other was of people on surfboards happily riding on breaking waves.

She felt straightaway that the water was an image of the Holy Spirit, as several times in the Bible. So on reflection the pictures present alternative responses to God working by the Spirit, including the whole matter of God speaking to people by his Spirit. People can basically dislike it. Or it can be a sphere which they learn to navigate without fear and find to be full of freedom and exhilaration.

9. EVANGELISM

The hope that is in us

An image remains with me from a period of time in the 1980s when I was in secular employment and worked in the computer department of a Mail Order Company. Four of us were working together one morning in a particular office when entirely unexpectedly one of the others, a young woman in her late twenties, decided to sit on top of her desk instead of behind it. From this position she announced to anyone who might be interested that she simply did not know what life was really all about. She said she regularly woke up in the night and wondered about it.

She was impelled to a moment of complete honesty. She was a capable and sociable person. She did not generally behave in an eccentric way or give any impression of not coping with life's demands.

Not everyone necessarily experiences ultimate questions with such intensity. Many who do feel the force of ultimate questions do not necessarily expect religion to provide satisfying answers. But when the questions are raised in daily life it does matter that Christians should respond. Sometimes we may feel we have offered the best we could and sometimes not. It is good if what we say has some quality that might carry on working in their mind when they are awake at three o'clock in the morning.

Evangelism, which is the theme of innumerable books, has already been a theme of this one. Not all Christians are natural evangelists but all of us have to say something on occasion. We cannot foretell the possible significance of what we say. I know a man who had been a convinced atheist for years of his adult life, allowing his wife to take the children to Sunday School but fiercely resistant of according Christianity any truth whatever. One day on the top of a bus two schoolgirls were sitting behind him, chatting together quietly about some things which were happening at their church. He turned round and said, 'You don't believe in all that stuff, do you?' One of them answered straightforwardly , 'Yes we do - what do you believe in?' He described how even as a hardened non-believer he felt as though he had been punched in the stomach. The effect was not merely momentary. Next morning when he woke up he knew there was a God.

The First Letter of Peter carries a basic instruction for Christian witness. 'In your hearts sanctify Christ as Lord. Always be ready to make your defence to anyone who demands from you a reason for the hope that is in you; yet do it with gentleness and respect' (3.15-16). Peter knew that his readers here might regularly be faced with misunderstanding and hostile accusations. But it remains a significant instruction for Christians in our twenty-first century society with its widespread effective disassociation from the Church and its pick-and-mix attitude to all sorts of spiritual possibilities.

There are three elements in this text.

First, there is reverence for Jesus as Lord. He is risen from the dead and he is Lord. What he claims and what he offers are relevant to everybody. One commentator on this passage describes this reverence as 'a respectful awe focused on Christ, that drives out other fears and makes possible an honest and effective response to interrogation'.[1]

Second, there is the readiness to talk naturally about our conviction. Readiness is important. Often we need to bother less about creating opportunities than about meeting the ones that come anyway. Many of us can be so scared of appearing pushy that we simply lose chances to offer others the help and stimulation they seek, at least to point them in some direction. Naturalness is vital. People easily sense if we are tense or have to talk about faith in a different way to talking about normal things. We certainly don't have to pretend to know everything.

Thirdly, we should consistently treat others with gentleness and respect. We should treat them as we would like to be treated and listen to what they are saying. We are open to learn from others and sense how God may already be leading them. We should never impose too much detail of our own experience unless they are interested in hearing it. In any case our own experience cannot be imposed on them. They need to encounter God for themselves.

Although the gentleness and respect are vital the reverence for Jesus is primary. *God engages intimately with his Church when it says to others, 'Jesus is the Bread of Life. Without him we perish'. The Church should see itself as though surrounded by crowds of spiritually starving, emaciated people. The Church questions God: 'How may we reach this multitude?' God answers, 'Not by a plan but by a passion'.*

We can calculate how powerful would be the effect if any of us by personal influence could every year draw one other person into

100

Christian commitment, giving them also sufficient encouragement that in following years they would be able to do the same. The principle of multiplication would result after ten years in over a thousand committed Christians and after twenty years in over a million. Some extraordinary multiplication effects do occur in times and places when church growth is running high.

We know that for any one individual we encounter we cannot determine what may happen this year, next year or in eight years' time. In a book of essays on evangelism a theologian called David Clark tells of a lawyer who he happened to meet through a mutual friend.[2] He had some conversation with him about Christianity. This man showed instinctive scepticism towards religious institutions and theological claims. As a matter of integrity he dropped church attendance long ago, even though his wife and in-laws still went.

David talked to him about some of the arguments for Christianity and especially the way that moral law points to a transcendent Creator, whom we ought to seek. George replied, 'Yes, I see your perspective and it's a good one. It makes a lot of sense to you. But I prefer to take a more moderate, agnostic position'. He was typical of many people today who have some spiritual interest but also a distrust of institutions and a preference against commitment.

Eight years later David found out that George had returned to church and that after several months of attending worship he had expressed personal commitment to Jesus Christ.

What made the difference? Not my conversation with him, I'm sure. Nor any other one thing, I suspect. I'd say the Holy Spirit used a loving wife, a couple of philosophical insights, a long-term friendship with a Christian man, the experience of the worshipping church, some precision on theological understanding and the eternity tucked inside his heart. [3]

He makes light of the significance of his own conversation. But it is still important that we can say something about the hope that is in us. What are the reasons for the hope that is in me? I accept scientific understanding, including the processes of evolution, but I do not believe that human life with all its qualities has no other level of explanation. I cannot evade the claim of Jesus to show us the true meaning of our lives through personally knowing the God whom he reveals. I cannot dismiss the evidence for Easter and that it was a unique event by which this God said a resounding Yes to the mission

101

of Jesus. And I am one of countless people of all sorts whose experience of seeking God through Jesus gives confidence in encouraging others to do so.

Tendencies of our time

Sometimes I have used the following outline when encouraging those in local churches to think about the trends in contemporary society and the nature of Christian responses. Although there are many varieties of tendency and 'culture' even in one particular country these are at least some aspects of a generally recognisable picture. There is no claim to completeness here and there is no particular order in the list.[4]

- Globalisation. Speed of communication can make the world seem a small place, major companies operate across national boundaries, Coca-Cola is everywhere.
- Consumerism. Shopping is a major leisure activity. Large shopping centres are a modern equivalent to cathedrals and advertising often borrows the language of worship. (Consumer standards frustrate those who can't afford more and can create massive debts).
- Electronics. Computerisation and the Internet, with new ways of amassing and processing information. Proliferation of screen entertainment.
- Images. Constant emphasis on personal appearance. Advertising supplies images to encourage shopping. Images can become a substitute for thought.
- Relativism. Loss of expectation of finding absolute truth. 'OK if it works for you....' Right of personal freedom to choose in every area.
- The present. Loss of traditional roots. Loss of confidence in science or politics to deliver secure hope for the future. Loss of substantial hope for anything beyond death. Therefore: tendency to concentrate on the present and 'feel-good' experiences now.
- Fragmentation. Individualism and limited loyalties. Conflicts between people of different 'tribes'. Desire for intimacy but difficulties of keeping committed relationships and breakdown of family stabilities. Increase of litigation, looking for someone to blame.

- Spiritual quest. Openness to many sorts of spirituality. Only 10 per cent of the adult population in Britian are now in church even once a month, though many more would call themselves Christian. Spiritual hunger but aversion to institutions.

Of course it is possible not to present this outline ready-made but to ask a group of Christians to say what they think are the trends and then to think together about the Christian perspectives. A few Bible texts are quoted here but only as representative of the Bible's richness and range.

- Globalisation. 'God so loved the world....' (John 3.16) The world is the object of love of a transcendent God who has revealed himself supremely in one human life in particular time and place.
- Consumerism. We can rightly and thankfully enjoy all sorts of things (1 Tim.4.5), keeping them in their proper place and practising contentment and sacrifice as well (Phil. 4.11). Major Christian imperatives in our own time are the alleviation of world poverty and the conservation of the planet's resources.
- Electronics. The Church needs to make the most of new technology, though not subordinating substance to presentation. We need wisdom to help us judge knowledge (1 Cor.2.6).
- Images. Appearance is not all. God looks at the heart (1 Sam. 16.7) We are not to be tied to devotion to 'images' (1 John 5.21)
- Relativism. Christianity does offer absolute truths and standards, though often needing to be applied in specific situations with the Holy Spirit's help. Freedom to serve Christ and others is real freedom (John 8.36).
- The present. We can have deep roots in Scripture and Christian history. We can have present-day hope for seeing God at work, even in a suffering world (Rom. 15.13). Heaven is our ultimate hope of unimaginable fulfilment in God's presence (1 Pet. 1.3,4).
- Fragmentation. We can learn authentic Christian love and its power to restore and bless relationships. We can have individuality along with real mutual interdependence (1 Cor. 12.12).
- Spiritual quest. We can find the true meaning of our life in personal relationship with God through Jesus and in belonging to living Christian communities.

For many today God is merely question mark or exclamation mark, a mental puzzle or a thoughtless expletive. For Christians also he is question mark and exclamation mark (Romans 11.33-36), in the different sense of deep mystery and real marvel. We do not pretend to fathom the answers to all the questions but neither are we condemned to total agnosticism (not knowing anything about what matters most), because we believe in a God who has chosen to reveal himself.

The Alpha course

'Not by a plan but by a passion'. I know I am not offering a plan nor a story of personal achievement. But I would like to comment on our experiences of using the Alpha course. Between 1994 and 2004, in three local church situations in different parts of England, my wife and I encouraged the running of Alpha and gave a lead part in the practical organisation.

Alpha was a success story of mission in the 1990s. Its birthplace was the Anglican parish church of Holy Trinity Brompton in a prosperous central area of London. The course offers an introduction to the Christian faith with weekly sessions for about ten weeks. Typically an Alpha evening begins with a shared meal, continues with a talk on a Christian theme and concludes with small group discussion. Material for the course is provided by literature which is readily available.[5] Often videos of the talks given at HTB by Nicky Gumbel have been used as the main content in other places. By the end of the decade Alpha was being run by over 6000 churches in Britain of variety of denominations and by thousands more worldwide

We were glad of chances to use Alpha. We regularly encouraged church members to go through it both for their own sake and in the hope that it might encourage them later to invite others whom they knew. We enjoyed creating the environment where those who were already church members could meet on friendly terms with those whose church connections were much slighter, maybe having simply responded to a poster on an external noticeboard. We enjoyed getting to know individuals better both in the leisurely context of eating a meal together week by week and in the small-group conversations. The courses embraced variety of ages from teenage to elderly and people at all sorts of junctures in their own lives. We appreciated the elements of team co-operation in the practical aspects of running the course.

Our own experience in three places was that significant numbers of church members genuinely welcomed it as a 'refresher'. Significant numbers of those who were not church members stayed the duration of the course and professed to have been helped, often with a new or renewed sense of the personal reality and love of God. Sometimes these were joined to the life of our own or another church in an ongoing way. Others who testified to having found help from God as a significant step in moving on with their lives seemed to preserve it as something personal within their own circumstances. One young wife had a husband who did not mind her doing Alpha on a weekday evening but would not countenance her giving time to church at weekends. The experience of running Alpha can therefore highlight questions about the varied forms of church life which need to be offered.

We have believed in Alpha as a concept and still do. This is not to elevate a particular course as containing the total answer for evangelisation in contemporary society. Any course is only as good as by God's help we can make it. In the case of Alpha wise leadership in the small groups is specially important.

Alpha can be tailored to circumstance. We did use it in our own way in particular aspects and these may be worth mentioning.

We rarely used the videos in entirety. When running the course in one church we used only live input by which a variety of competent local people took turns to deliver the substance of the talk. Subsequently we tended to use a mixture of Nicky Gumbel on video (whatever seemed to me the most striking 20 minutes of his 40-minute talk) and live input from myself to cover the rest. However, it is interesting that even if no preacher is ideal for everybody many do respond well to Nicky Gumbel's style and would gladly hear him at full length.

This approach allowed some variation in the handling of themes. For example, I would treat the question of the inspiration of the Bible with a stronger emphasis on the human authorship and the reflection of culture and provisional understandings of God, while also still arguing for the historical reliability of the New Testament record and showing utmost respect for the biblical witness as our primary means of understanding God's revelation.

Rather than attempting a full scale residential weekend in the middle of the course we arranged a Saturday afternoon event. This included the space for personal prayer for the Holy Spirit's help and blessing. In the HTB material on the Holy Spirit there is a particular section on speaking in tongues which we avoided as a main issue, choosing to emphasise the variety of ways that people might be conscious of God's presence and the Spirit's work.

It is the practice at HTB to include an element of worship on each evening and allow even uncommitted people to experience a worship atmosphere for short periods of time. Our own choice was to invite people simply to listen to a recorded piece of music as a transition from the mealtime to the spoken input. We used Christian songs by singers like Michael Card which had a biblical content and an attractive modern quality.

The originators of Alpha have said they are pleased for it to be varied according to local needs and sensibilities. However, they do not encourage trying to run it without the food! Whether Alpha is the best option in a particular local situation is a matter for churches to decide. Plenty of other courses are available to provide an introduction to Christianity and offer help in reading and understanding the Bible. But the principles of Alpha are capable of wide application in church life and outreach, whether or not Alpha itself is being used.

- Relationships based on friendship have always provided a context for evangelism and this is the natural environment in which people today will best consider the claims of Christianity afresh.

- Christian faith has a content which can be presented for consideration. The possibility of meaningful and transforming personal relationship with God through Jesus is consistently offered.

- There is at best a relaxed willingness to listen to the experience and questions of others, to let them withdraw from the course any time if they wish, to allow them what space and time they may need to come to terms with what is offered.

- There is an expectancy of God working in ways that cannot be predicted at the outset.

Spreading the table

Church services can be awful. Large numbers of people have been terminally put off Christianity by occasions of worship that lacked vitality of any kind and in no way reflected the power of Biblical revelation to bring us into contact with the God who created us. All of us who are responsible for the leading of worship must regularly review what we are offering.

What people find meaningful in worship will vary according to many factors, including the level of their Christian understanding and commitment, their theological or musical preferences, their love of service-book liturgy or their aversion to it. I am not pleading for frantic attempts at artificial enlivenment at the expense of serious teaching or quiet reflective spaces. But in some services practically anything by way of enlivenment would be welcome.

Many churches no longer expect uncommitted newcomers to appear. In any case evangelism today cannot depend only on inviting people to come to church and telling them they'll be welcome. But it is wonderful when a church, larger or smaller, inspires confidence in its members that it is worth inviting their friends, neighbours and acquaintances. 'It's so good at our church. You must come'. It is good when every time of worship, even if it is not specially oriented to the non-committed, has a capacity to convey to a seeking person the reality and love of God.

We cannot simply organise for worship to be like this. It is an aspect of the Church's ongoing cry to God, 'What you want to find in us, create in us'. Yet our planning is involved as well.

In my final year at the Methodist church in the town centre of Chesterfield in Derbyshire I asked that for a period of three full months, between New Year and Easter 2004, we might plan the main Sunday morning services with advertised themes. We would give special attention to messages being presented in a clear and relevant way and the whole content of worship being lively, using variety of music, pieces of film or interview or drama, and planned input by different church members that illustrated the living out of Christian commitment in the real world.

Even though we produced a publicity leaflet for these months new people did not flock in. But I felt God's own pleasure in the endeavour. Many of the services were a strong expression of the attractiveness of Christian truth, within a setting of worship clearly focused on God himself. Worship on Education Sunday included a lively presentation from a group who regularly went into Primary Schools to lead assemblies. Later a church member who was an education advisor spoke on issues facing teachers in schools today, the kind of relevant Christian comment that translates readily into prayer. A group of teenagers offered a 'diary of a week at school'. It presented the pressures experienced by young Christians in the school environment and also the rewards of knowing they had a solid basis for life and finding others responsive to that sometimes.

An instruction to 'spread the table' came repeatedly into my prayers before and during this time. God likes it when we spread the table with food which is good for us to eat and available for others to come in and share. For Heather the image of a large cooking pot vividly recurred. She knew it was full of delicious ingredients all boiling up together. Beyond this current project of our church's life, and whatever the limitations of its success, the cooking pot was an image of God's whole recipe for the life of his people, nutritious, satisfying, ready to be ladled out.

It is good news that God loves and accepts our desire to reach out to others with the Christian message, regardless of the results we see. Often it calls for great patience and perseverance. But neither must we limit what new things may develop for any of us or for any of our churches as we pray, 'Lord, do what you want to do! Reach those you want to reach!'.

Evangelism is a function of the life of Christian communities in their totality. There is an ancient report that Luke had artistic ability and painted a striking portrait of the Virgin Mary. We certainly know that he could paint pictures with words. At the end of the second chapter of the Acts of the Apostles he depicts the earliest Christian community in Jerusalem in a few skilful strokes (Acts 2. 42-47). It is a community marked by joyful worship, loving relationships, apostolic teaching, eucharistic meals, constant prayerfulness, awe-inspiring evidences of God's presence, sacrificial generosity, openness for others to come in.

Luke does not try to show this early church as a model of complete perfection. In chapter 6 he will mention how tension arose between different linguistic groups and needed wise resolution. But his picture in chapter 2 captures vivid memories of the quality of life experienced in the aftermath of Pentecost. Some aspects of that time were only temporary - leadership by the original apostles, the presence of Jesus' own mother and brothers, the continued attendance at the Temple services. But the overall depiction has had constant relevance to times and places of renewal throughout Christian history.

I have turned Luke's words into a version which can be sung and rises into a prayer for our own time [6]:

> They met repeatedly to share,
>   To celebrate their risen Head,
> To join in harmony of prayer,
>   Together eat the broken bread.
>
> They felt the closeness of the Lord,
>   Their hearts were gently touched with awe,
> So strong the presence they adored,
>   So great the wonders that they saw.
>
> They heard the first apostles teach
>   And worship made their spirits glad;
> To satisfy the needs of each
>   They sacrificed what each they had.
>
> Whatever those around might say,
>   And some approve and some oppose,
> They knew God's blessing every day
>   And every day their number rose.
>
> Come, Holy Spirit, as at first,
>   Come, Holy Spirit, and make clear
> The satisfaction of our thirst,
>   God's future kingdom present here.

THE FINAL APPEAL

WHEN I studied classics at University I attended seminars conducted by a professor well past retirement age, whose reputation still brought him a crowd of attentive hearers. He was extremely learned and also very kindly. Individual students were entrusted with sections of the material for advance preparation. I remember that more than once he excused a glaring failure on somebody's part to prepare thoroughly by observing quietly, 'non omnia possumus omnes', meaning 'we cannot all do everything'. This was generous because the division of work meant that nobody had actually been asked to do everything. They had only been asked to cover a particular item well.

As Christians we cannot all do everything but some things we must all do. In Paul's letter to the Christians in Rome there is a famous appeal in chapter 12 where he calls them all, in the light of God's mercy, to fresh dedication. 'Do not be conformed to this world but be transformed by the renewal of your minds, so that you may discern what is the will of God - what is good and acceptable and perfect' (Romans 12.2).

The appeal is in the light of God's mercy, which has been the whole theme of Paul's letter so far. God has not loved us abstractly from heaven but his love has been expressed on earth through the mission of Jesus and his self-giving at infinite cost. All of us are to be in touch with the mercy of God, get in touch with it, stay in touch with it. The scale of this mercy is measured by the central events on which Christian faith hangs - the Cross, the Resurrection, the outpouring of the Spirit.

We feel the limitations of our understanding. God knows we do. But he wants our dedication. He wants our worship. He wants to transform us. He wants to keep renewing our minds. He wants to give us fresh understanding of his will for us.

- Ask him to show you what he wants to show you, in the way that he wants to show it.

- Ask him to do what he wants to do with you, in the way that he wants to do it.

- Ask him to do what he wants with his Church, which remains his primary instrument in making known his truth and love through Jesus.

Within the scope of Paul's appeal in Romans 12 I offer again the things which God has spoken into my own prayers, as described in the first chapter.

God wants to stress the desire to please him, even where people feel they don't know exactly what pleases him. They are to cry, 'Show us what is pleasing to you'. God searches people's hearts and clears a way for himself.

In Romans 12 Paul uses the imagery of the human body to bring out the range and interdependence of gifts and calling. Knowing that Christians belong to one another in one body controls exaggerated ideas of anyone's status (v.3). 'Non omnia possumus omnes'. There is always variety in the way God shapes us and uses us. But Paul moves on again to things we must all do. 'Let love be sincere; hate what is evil; hold fast to what is good; love one another with mutual affection; outdo one another in showing honour. Do not flag in zeal, be set on fire by the Spirit, serve the Lord....' (vv. 9-12). His rapid imperatives outline a Christian calling where ardent passion is united with loving attitudes and actions and rational dedication to God's purposes.

> Do not flag in zeal.
> Be set on fire by the Spirit.
> Serve the Lord.
> Rejoice in hope.
> Bear up under suffering.
> Persist in prayer.

Persist in prayer! An Old Testament scholar, writing about the Psalms, says that whether they are exuberant with praise or groaning with hurt they are spoken to 'a named, known, addressable, reachable You'.[1] He quotes an old Jewish prayer which begins:

> *Where I wander – You!*
> *Where I ponder – You!*
> *Only You, You again, always You!*
> *You! You! You!*

112

In the light of everything I have written, I urge you to pray for the renewal of the Church in these terms —

Holy Spirit, your power!
Jesus Christ, your passion!
Lord God, your purposes!

NOTES

Chapter 1 - The purpose of God

1. Pete Greig and Dave Roberts, *Red Moon Rising*, Kingsway, 2004. See further in chapter 8.
2. Other examples beside the one mentioned: Martin Robinson and Dwight Smith, *Invading Secular Space*, Monarch, 2003; *Mission-Shaped Church*, Church House Publishing, 2004; Steven Croft and others, *Evangelism in a Spiritual Age*, Church House Publishing, 2005.
3   Bob Jackson, *Hope for the Church*, Church House Publishing, 2002, p. xi.
4   Jackson, p.185.

Chapter 2 - The passion of Jesus

1. Jurgen Moltmann, *Trinity and the Kingdom*, Fortress, 1993, p. 23.
2   Kenda Creasy Dean, *Practicing Passion*, Eerdmans, 2004.
3. Isobel Kuhn, *By Searching*.
4   Wayne Grudem, *Systematic Theology*, Zondervan, 1994, pp. 867-9.
5. Rick Warren, *The Purpose Driven Church*, Zondervan,1995.

Chapter 3 - The Spirit's empowering

1. The setting is described in detail by Alfred Edersheim, *The Life and Times of Jesus the Messiah*, Book 4, Ch.7.
2. This is discussed by Colin Gunton, *Father, Son and Holy Spirit*, T and T Clark, 2003, pp. 8-11.
3. Catherine Marshall, *Something More*, Hodder, 1974. Quotations are from pp. 279-284.
4. Ed. Mark Elsdon-Dew, *The Collection*, HTB Publications,1996, pp. 185f.
5. Gordon Fee, *God's Empowering Presence*, Hendrickson,1994, p. 896f.
6. Quotations in what follows are from pp. 901f (used with permission).
7. James Dunn, *Jesus and the Spirit*, SCM, 1975, p. 360.
8. Thomas Aquinas, *Summa Theologiae*, q. 43.

Chapter 4 - The large picture

1. Fred Wright, *The Cross became a Sword*, Reconciliation Walk Publishing, 1995.
2. William Lane, *The Gospel of Mark*, Eerdmans, 1974, pp.449-50.
3. Gerard Kelly and Lowell Sheppard, *Miracle in Mostar*, Lion, 1995, p.125.
4 Noel Dermot O'Donoghue, *Aristocracy of Soul: Patrick of Ireland*, Darton Longman and Todd, 1987. This includes full translation of the 'Confession', pp. 101-118.
5. O'Donoghue, p. 53

Chapter 5 – God and Methodism

1. Journal of Charles Wesley for February 24th 1738.
2. Journal of John Wesley for May 24th 1738.
3. Taken from Martin Robinson and Dwight Smith, *Invading Secular Space*, Monarch, 2003, p. 67.
4. The whole story is recently explored by David Hempton, *Methodism, Empire of the Spirit*, Yale University, 2005.
5 These examples are taken from Leslie Church, *Early Methodist People*, Epworth, 1948, pp. 113-116 for Henry Longden and pp. 13-15 for Sarah Bentley.
6. Randy Maddox, *Responsible Grace: John Wesley's Practical Theology*, Kingswood Books, 1994, pp. 126-7.
7. John Vincent, *Christ and Methodism*, Epworth, 1960s.
8. Richard Jones and Anthony Wesson, *Towards a Radical Church*, Epworth, 1970, pp. 66f. (used with permission)
9. Jones and Wesson, pp. 70-76.
10 Maddox, as above.
11. *Priorities for the Methodist Church* (report of the 'Where are we heading?' consultation process).
12 *An Anglican-Methodist Covenant*, published by Methodist Publishing House and Church House Publishing, 2001.

Chapter 6 - Remembering the twentieth century

1. This is from the Foreword of Barth's *Christian Dogmatics*, Munich, 1927.
2. Barth, *The Word of God and the Word of Man*, pp. 195f .

3   Gordon Rupp, *The Old Reformation and the New,* Epworth, 1967, p. 55.

4.   Quotations from the chapter 'God's Only Son' in Karl Barth, *Dogmatics in Outline,* SCM, 1949, pp. 73-8.

5.   Barth, *Dogmatics in Outline,* p. 130.

6.   Barth, *Evangelical Theology: An Introduction,* p. 58.

7.   This account of Azusa Street is indebted to Jean-Jacques Suurmond, *Word and Spirit at Play,* SCM, 1994, pp. 1-6.

8.   Patrick Johnstone and Jason Mandryk, *Operation World,* Paternoster, 2001, p. 3.

9   Jose Comblin, *The Holy Spirit and Liberation,* Orbis, 1989, p. 20

10   The account of John Wimber's life in the following paragraphs is based primarily on his video 'I'm a Fool for Christ', Mercy Publishing, 1987. His wife Carol wrote his biography as *The Way it Was,* Hodder, 1999.

11.   Wimber with Kevin Springer, *Power Evangelism ,* Hodder, 1985, revised 1992; *Power Healing,* Hodder, 1986.

12.   Wimber, *Living with Uncertainty,* Vineyard Ministries International, 1996.

13.   Ed. John Arnott, *Experience the Blessing,* Renew Books, 2000.

Chapter 7 - 'Lord, teach us to pray'

1.   Brother Yun with Paul Hattaway, *The Heavenly Man,* Monarch, 2002. The story of the prayer for a Bible pp.26-30.

2.   Sally Phillips, 'Like a spare salad bowl', in the magazine *Third Way,* June 2002.

3   Yun, pp. 299f.

4.   John Wesley records it in his Journal on this date.

5.   Quotations in this section are from Greig and Roberts, *Red Moon Rising,* and from the website www.24-7prayer.com

6.   Renewal in the Cuban Methodist Church more fully described by Leo Osborn in 'Country of Contradictions' in *Methodist Recorder,* May 26th 2005. Quotation from Bishop Pereira Draz taken from www.worldmethodist.org

7.   Ed. Mark Elsdon-Dew, *The Collection,* HTB Publications, 1996, pp. 185f.

8   John Wimber, *Prayer: Intimate Communication with God,* Vineyard Ministries International, 1997.

Chapter 8 - Listening to God

1. Website at www.voiceinthedesert.org.uk
2. For some of the material in this section I am indebted to Klaus Bockmuehl, *Listening to the God who Speaks*, Helmers and Howard, 1990.
3. Randy Maddox, *Responsible Grace: John Wesley's Practical Theology*, Kingswood Books, 1994, p.135.
4. Jack Deere, *Surprised by the Voice of God*, Kingsway, 1996.

Chapter 9 - Evangelism

1. Ramsey Michaels, *1 Peter (Word Biblical Commentary 49)*, Word Books, 1988, p. 187.
2. David K. Clark, Postmodern Evangelical Apologetics, in ed. S.W.Chung, *Alister E. McGrath and Evangelical Theology*, Paternoster, 2003, pp. 310-2.
3. Clark, p. 332.
4. Though the overall formulation is my own here I think I owe some of the phrases to hearing a talk by Graham Cray who is an expert on post-modern culture.
5. Nicky Gumbel's talks for the Alpha course published as *Questions of Life*, Kingsway, 1993.
6. Any suitable LM tune, perhaps 'Sweet Harmony' (Handel Parker).

The final appeal

1. Walter Brueggemann, *The Psalms and the Life of Faith*, Fortress, 1995, p. 37. He quotes the prayer from Martin Buber, *Tales of the Hasidim: The Early Masters*, Schocken, 1947, p. 212.

Printed in the United Kingdom
by Lightning Source UK Ltd.
107666UKS00003B/1-96